WHAT WORKS

WHAT WORKS

*The Ten Best Ideas
from the First 200 Episodes*

CAM MARSTON

What Works: The Ten Best Ideas from the First 200 Episodes

For information about this title or to order other books
and/or electronic media, contact the publisher:

Marston Communications
PO Box 81118
Mobile, Alabama 36689
www.CamMarston.com
info@CamMarston.com

ISBNs:
979-8-9860067-0-3 (softcover)
979-8-9860067-1-0 (eBook)

Printed in the United States of America

Cover and Interior design: 1106 Design

This book is dedicated to the memory of Judy Marston.

In the process of writing this book, I lost my mother. She was instrumental in getting my speaking business started over twenty years ago. She and I partnered to give presentations, sharing the stage, discussing the generational issues that were perplexing business leaders at the time. I went on to a solo career when she decided to retire. That foundation led to opportunities for me to write books, record videos, travel the world, and begin the *What's Working with Cam Marston* radio broadcast and podcast, and so many other things. I was excited for the day that I would bring the first copy of this book through my parents' front door and give it to her with a heartfelt thanks and a hug for being my catalyst to what's been a wonderful career and life. That day won't happen and I'm heartbroken about it. I'll miss her terribly.

CONTENTS

ACKNOWLEDGMENTS

*J*ohnny Gwin runs Deep Fried Studios and is the knobs and dials guy whenever I record in-person versus over the phone. He is, however, much more than a knobs-and-dials guy. His insights into how to frame a question and his vast areas of expertise and innumerable connections have helped me immeasurably, and he has become a friend.

Kristin Ogden was instrumental in getting *What's Working with Cam Marston* off the ground and gaining traction. She screened guests, scheduled interviews, and worked social media. There is no way the show would have hit the two-hundred-episode mark without her.

As General Manager of FMTalk106.5, Sean Sullivan offered me a chance to create a radio show by offering me time on his station. He gave me a shot. He's answered my countless questions and has encouraged me to continue on my path and complimented me when my confidence needed boosting. He's a role model as a broadcaster and is the best one I know.

John Thompson is the producer for *What's Working with Cam Marston*. Of those that are instrumental to the show's success and whatever longevity it has and will have, John's at the top of the list. His company is EyeOn Digital and he makes each show's timing work; regardless of how hard I try to make it difficult on him, he gets the show ready for broadcast each week and finds solutions to every hiccup I can throw his way. He's been a shoulder when I need one and the best motivator I've ever had. The show exists today because of my partnership and friendship with John.

Helen Broder has historically been my business manager for my speeches, workshops and seminars. Today she's jumped in to helping with *What's Working* when COVID eliminated travel, causing much of my seminar business to come to a halt. She's been an advocate for me and my talents for over ten years and is one of the most honest and ethical businesspeople I've ever worked with. I cherish our friendship.

Steven James and I have worked together on past book projects and I brought him in on this one to help with some final ideas and edits. He knows the way I think and the quality of the product I aspire to present and has, once again, done a bang-up job. When we're together and I'm pitching an idea and he's rocking back and forth, I know he's thinking excitedly. When I asked him to help with this project over lunch one day, he started rocking and I knew he was interested and, thankfully, he offered to pitch in.

Betty Darby made the book happen. Her speed on this project was truly exceptional. She helped with each chapter and presented options along the way when she saw different ways of telling the stories. She offered direction and gladly took direction when I felt something different needed emphasis. She was an organized soldier and never wavered when I went AWOL a few times when different things in my other worlds needed my attention. Simply put, this book would not be in existence if it were not for Betty. Thank you, Betty.

Lisa Marston is my wife of well over twenty years. She must wonder sometimes how she got to Mobile, Alabama from Raleigh, North Carolina with a husband who has an idea for a radio show, does public radio commentaries, travels giving speeches, and now has four kids and a dog. She suffers through hunting season, fishing season, Mardi Gras season, and on and on. I'm sure her crystal ball never predicted anything like this. However, I'm the most grateful man in the world that she took a liking to me and continues to support me through all of it. Thankfully, she's steadfast. She's never flinched. We work together to make sure each other's life is neither predictable nor boring.

INTRODUCTION

*W*hat Works?

What's the difference between a business that succeeds and one that fails? Between one that succeeds and one that soars? How do we define success and what attributes does it take to achieve it? Where do the ideas come from that launch flourishing businesses and what is the formula for sustaining them? These are the questions in the minds of everyone who starts or runs a business, and finding the answers can be a matter of survival. According to the U.S. Department of Labor, almost half of all businesses fail in the first five years. Two-thirds are gone before ten years. Only 25 percent make it to fifteen. So, finding out "what works" is vital.

Beyond survival, most would like to achieve financial security for themselves, their families, and their employees. And beyond financial rewards, most of us would like to find meaning and fulfillment, even happiness, in our work. What's the secret to putting all this together in our companies and careers? Or is it really a secret at all?

"What works" is the subject of my radio show, *What's Working with Cam Marston*. The premise of the show is simple. Each week, we have a guest who owns or runs a successful enterprise, and we ask them, "What do you do?" and "How do you do it?" And then we listen. The answers aren't necessarily secrets, but a wonderful mix of inspiration, common sense, hard work, and determination. No grand theories but a lot of successful formulas.

Many of the best business books wrestle with these issues by closely examining the most successful enterprises. Jim Collins' landmark *Good to Great* compares firms that are merely "good" with those that achieved greatness and tries to identify what made the difference. Others, like Malcolm Gladwell, look at extraordinary individuals and the special traits that set them apart. In my case, I have deployed my boundless curiosity (more on this later). I like to ask questions. I am fascinated by what makes entrepreneurs and their businesses tick. When I come across someone who has "made it," no matter what field they're in, I just have to ask, "How did you do it?"

I have done that now for two hundred episodes of *What's Working,* and the answers have both delighted and enlightened me and, I hope, our audience. I have interviewed a wide variety of professionals, and their answers and experiences have been even more varied. However, after two hundred episodes, I could see some patterns emerge and some common threads that ran through all the success stories. This book collects those threads—the best *ideas* to emerge from the show.

CASE STUDIES IN SUCCESS

The chapters follow a thread from founding a business to sustaining it to passing it on, and the best ideas to emerge from our interviews are presented here as a series of case studies. Each case study focuses on a single successful business or entrepreneur that embodies a best business practice. These best practices, not surprisingly, are common to other success stories. Each chapter is focused on one of these best practices, best attributes, or best ideas. Here's what you'll find:

- → Ten chapters focused on the ten best ideas from the *What's Working* interviews

- → Ideas flow from starting up a business to keeping it successful to planning for the future

- → Each chapter features several case studies from *What's Working*

- → "What Works" takeaways follow each chapter

Taken together, this is a roadmap of the many paths to success—more like a road atlas (remember those?) than Google Maps directions. To me, the most compelling part of these case studies is that they come from real businesses succeeding in today's marketplace and from real people who were kind enough to sit down with us and share their stories.

(All the episodes are still available as podcasts if you would like to hear them yourself!)

TWO HUNDRED AND COUNTING

How did I get here, two hundred episodes later and still counting?

Well, I have a curiosity problem. I ask lots of questions. It can become an issue. My wife is fond of telling the story of when I was asked to get to the back of the line at a tour of the Biltmore House in Asheville, North Carolina. The tour guide told me I had already asked more questions than any other tour she'd ever given, we were already an hour behind schedule and were only in the second room of the tour. Another time I sat at a table with the offensive coordinator for the University of Alabama football team and asked him about how he and his staff structure their time in the off-season. About twenty minutes into our conversation and after lots of questions from me, he stopped me. He said that he's been interviewed by dozens of media folks in sports and has never been asked as many good questions as I had asked in our chat over barbecue waiting for the main speaker. I, simply put, like asking questions. It stems from a genuine interest in people, what they do, and why and how they do it.

Asking questions obviously leads to answers. But often for me, it's not just people's answers but the words they select while answering that tells me about them. Or how they articulate a certain word. Or where their eyes look or a subtle shift in their expression when they answer. It's not what they say, it's how they say what they say that teaches me about them and leads me to ask something different or to pick up on a cue that makes me think there's something else there and there's another question I need to ask. I have no interest in trapping someone through a trick question. I have no vendetta, nor do I hope to spring a "gotcha" question and make them regret saying something. It's truly my interest in them. My interest in learning about what they do and why they do it. My interest in—to use an overused phrase—what makes them "tick."

When I brought my idea for a radio show to Mobile, Alabama's FMTalk106.5 General Manager Sean Sullivan, I had no idea what I was getting into or what would happen. I had about fifty show ideas outlined, with proposed guests who I knew or who I knew of that would make a good expert for the topic. Sean said he'd not seen a show proposal with that much detail before and he'd be willing to give my show a try. Sean has since become a great ally of mine and of *What's Working with Cam Marston* and, I'm proud to say, a friend. He's been more than fair with me as I've asked for his criticisms and have tried to learn this craft. It is a craft, by the way, that he's mastered.

The first show I recorded was with the University of North Carolina volleyball coach Joe Sagula, asking him if he's having to recruit this new generation of volleyball player any differently than he had to in the past. I was a train wreck. Joe answered each question wonderfully well, and I eventually took some clips of his comments and played them in speeches I was giving to prove my point: This next generation was going to be different in the workplace because coaches were having to alter their recruiting tactics with this generation to find success. Joe's experiences were leading indicators of what the workplace would get in a few more years. Joe was great. But my management of that first interview was awful. I can't listen to it. In fact, for the first six months I refused to interview anyone in person because I didn't feel I could manage the interview well without my face in a pile of notes. Furthermore, I was afraid eye contact with my guest would throw off my train of thought. I created a makeshift studio in my home office to interview via phone—people who lived and worked down the street from me.

THE BEST IDEAS

But my guests' ideas came through. I heard them loud and clear. And I tried to highlight their ideas back to them in each interview to make the point to the listener. The show's focus is workplace, workforce, and marketplace trends, and I try to pull those trends out of my guests. I want my listener to be interested in the person I'm interviewing, learn something from the interview, and be able to apply what they've learned to their own life—work or personal—in some way or another.

And some ideas keep coming through. The same ones over and over. Worded differently by each guest, but the same concepts. And it's those ideas that are the focus of this book. This book isn't highlighting the ten best *interviews*, it's highlighting the ten best *ideas*. Each of the ideas could have been used by several guests. Each idea comes from a business owner or business leader who is doing their best to treat their employees and/or their customers right. These guests are often—but not always—thought leaders. They're often—but not always—empathetic people who want their customers or employees to feel something special about their company. They're often—but not always—dissatisfied with the way they're doing things, knowing it could be better. But guests are always grateful. Grateful for their customers, grateful for their employees, grateful for the opportunities they've been given through their job, their company, or their work. Just grateful people. That's been undeniably consistent.

So, this book highlights the ten best ideas I've heard since my first broadcast of *What's Working with Cam Marston* on February 28, 2018. This is not the type of book that would serve as a business school text. It's meant to be a light read for a busy businessperson who is looking for some ideas for their own business from others who have been there, done that, but admit they still have a long way to go and a lot to learn. The book is meant for the reader to ask, "I wonder if this idea is something my business could use? Or maybe it's an idea I can adopt for myself, personally." Whatever, my hope is that it stimulates your thoughts about what you are doing, what you have done, and what you could do differently. Goodness knows many of these ideas have become pivotal to my own business.

In the meantime, I'll keep at it. For the first year or so, I wasn't sure if I liked doing it or not. I worried so much about whether I could honor my guest appropriately and keep the interview going that I was a nervous wreck each time another interview would get close on my calendar. Now in my fourth year, I can honestly say that I love doing it. And calling people to ask them to be on the radio is fun, too. They're usually caught off guard and flattered. I've made great networking connections and more than a few new friends through many of the interviews, realizing that not only does my guest have a good story to tell, but I like them, too, and want to know them better. So, I'll keep at it. It's become an important part of my life. It's a joy. And it helps satisfy my deep, deep craving to ask questions.

After all, I have a curiosity problem . . .

1

PURSUE YOUR PASSION

Doing what you love can produce unique quality.

When I look at the business world today, I see growth and excitement on two opposite sides and not in the middle. On one side are the massive companies, the Amazons, the Walmarts, that can deliver volume, speed, convenience and uniformity, usually at a much lower price than their small competitors. On the other side, though, we have the boutique producers and servicers. Craft beer, the fad that became a niche that became a staple (a different staple in every market but still a staple), is a good example of the power of "boutique" appeal. The successful businesses at this end of the spectrum are usually driven by someone's *passion*.

Boutique hotels, boutique foodstuffs, boutique clothing lines and makeups, boutique whiskeys—you'll find them all across the retail and service sectors, usually at a premium price. Maybe they're cloaked in code words like "artisan" or "curated" or "small-batch," but you'll recognize a boutique product right away. And their success says that, while we are content with settling for mass-produced goods and experiences in most parts of our lives, we all have something we are willing to pay a premium for and to look harder for, something that must be absolutely the best, something that not everyone can or will buy.

When I was thinking through guests who would reflect passion-driven businesses, I kept finding my choices skewed toward those who are creating products and services in the boutique spectrum. There certainly are CEOs of behemoth corporations who are passionate about what they are doing—I know plenty of them. But passion-driven leaders are far easier to find when the word "boutique" applies to their business.

Case Study

OYSTERS ARE FOR LOVERS

SHOW TITLE: *Murder Point Oysters: The Story of a Bayou La Batre Shrimper Who Never Looked Back*

BROADCAST: *August 5, 2019*

You can taste the passion Lane Zirlott feels for his Murder Point Oysters. In fact, as he discusses the tasting notes of his farmed *Crassostrea virginica* oysters, Lane sounds more like a vintner discussing his prize wine than the former shrimper he is.

It's hardly surprising Lane turned to the sea for his livelihood—he's the fifth generation of his family to work the Gulf of Mexico. But a shrimper's life is a hard life, not only physically demanding but calling for long hours and extended absences—and those absences are particularly hard when there are children at home. When a visiting expert from Auburn University held a seminar on oyster aquaculture, Lane's mom noted that none of the area's commercial oystermen signed up and suggested that Lane attend. After checking out the possibilities, this Bayou La Batre shrimper embraced a change of product and a change of lifestyle.

"When we were in shrimp boats, you never knew you were getting any of my product," Lane says. "These oysters have a story. You find your favorite brand of oysters, like our Murder Point Oysters, and you follow them. Anybody can grow an oyster, but with these boutique oysters, you're raising them. It reflects in the end product. It makes you take pride in it—it's not like a commodity."

Those bags of clean, largely uniform oysters bear the Murder Point label like a signature, not unlike the label on that special bottle of wine you treat yourself to at a celebration. And Lane takes a paternal pride in their quality. And why not? He submerges the oysters on a long line in wire crates, a technique developed in Australia. He controls their depth—deeper means more nutrients, higher means fewer predators. He cranks them out of the water as much as 60 percent of a day, essentially training them to keep their shells closed—a valuable trait when it comes to taking them to market. He submerges them at high tide to get the greatest salinity. He determines when they are mature enough to harvest. In short, he crafts these mollusks and literally shapes how they taste.

Chances are you have heard wine aficionados wax poetic about "terroir," the word that sums up the combination of soil, climate, rock and elemental exposure on grapes and, ultimately, the wine they produce. Well, Lane tastes terroir in oysters. Murder Point oysters, grown as they are off a freshwater creek lined with Alabama pines and subject to twice-daily tidal incursion, have a naturally butter-like taste, he maintains. Choose oysters from any of the fifteen or so other oyster farms along Alabama's coast, and you'll get a different flavor profile, including one he describes as tasting faintly of mint.

"The gospel of the Southern oyster is the simple truth, and that truth is a Southern oyster can hold its own against any oyster on Earth. It deserves its place at the finest table at the finest restaurants anywhere," Lane says. "When you get into the flavor profile of oysters, don't give up on Southern oysters if you don't like one. They're different, so try another."

Let me pause here and say that yes, it is Murder Point Oyster Company. Murder as in "bloody mayhem." The area where the Zirlotts set up their oyster farm was once known as Myrtle Point, but a long-ago dispute over oyster rights led to a murder and the name changed. A bit macabre? Yes, but Lane goes with it, using the tagline "Oysters worth killing for" on his website.

The aquaculture process means the oysters never touch the muddy bottom and mature without collecting barnacles. The results are clean, uniform shells, Lane says. Small wonder they caught on, largely due to social media, which makes marketing a boutique product easier. Soon, the Zirlotts found they could not keep up with demand, in part because they couldn't purchase enough reliable "seed."

Oysters are living animals. They don't literally grow from seeds—but that's what immature oysters are called. To get seed, you put male and female oysters together in the right conditions and nurture the developing results, known as "spat," until they reach seed size. When Lane couldn't buy enough seed he began growing his own. Oysters breed well to the sounds of Percy Sledge, he adds. "When you start picking out the parents of your oysters, you can almost go overboard how much you can dial this oyster into what you want," he says.

Marketing his oysters to restaurants proved to be a challenge, since Murder Point Oysters are a premium-priced, handcrafted boutique product. "For a long time, the distributors had the purveyors in one hand and the restaurants in the other," Lane says.

Instead, Lane and his employees went around distributors. They'd load up bags of oysters and target the prime restaurants in New Orleans and later, Charleston. Ask for access to a top-tier chef in these cities and you wind up at the end of a long line. But walk in the back door of a restaurant, which Lane learned is generally unlocked, drop a sack of oysters on the nearest counter and start shucking? Well, folks noticed—and they tasted, too. Soon chefs were singing the praises of Murder Point oysters on social media. Now, the company sells between 2,600 and 3,000 dozen every week.

Lane Zirlott didn't go looking for oyster aquaculture—he sort of stumbled into it. But when he stumbled in, he knew he was home. He clearly takes a paternal pride in his product. And the best way to eat a Murder Point oyster? According to their papa, raw with just a tiny drop of lemon juice. That way, you'll taste the passion.

Case Study

DEFINITELY NOT UP IN SMOKE

SHOW TITLE: *More Cigar Smokers Today Than Ever. And Jeff Zeiders Knows How to Reach Them.*

RELEASE DATE: *June 24, 2019*

Which brings me to Jeff Zeiders and CigarClub.com.

Most people, especially Millennials and those younger than them, are taught to regard all tobacco as uniformly evil. But I love a good cigar on occasion, as a special event, in the right circumstances—and I'm far from alone. And I am not a nicotine addict, any more than enjoying a cold beer after a round of golf or an occasional sippin' whiskey makes you an alcoholic. Cigar smoking, which can only be done in a limited number of places these days, actually *lends* itself to moderation. (My wife calls my lovely cigars "wife-repellent sticks.")

Back to CigarClub. We're all familiar with subscription services that deliver special products each month. An early one was the Book-of-the-Month Club, but now there are lots of them: subscriptions will deliver a varied monthly supply of foreign snack foods, blooming bulbs, fashion, makeup, neckties, socks—you name it. Thanks to CigarClub, you can add cigars to that list. Jeff Zeiders and his partner were the first into the curated cigar subscription business, and others soon followed.

How does it work? Members sign up, take a short online quiz and get matched with a flavor profile picked by the club's algorithm. Based on the results, members get either three or five (depending on which they signed up for) cigars each month. Jeff figures they get the early flavor selections right about 95 percent of the time and make good on the ones members don't like. A thousand different customers are likely to result in a thousand completely different monthly cigar shipments. Meanwhile, each member's ratings and reviews sharpen the accuracy of their personal algorithm.

"We are asking people 'Do you drink coffee? What is your favorite type of beer? Wine? What is your go-to late-night snack or munchie? What are your favorite meats and proteins?'" Jeff says. The answers give the algorithm a starting point and the selection goes from there.

Along the way, they developed a totally new market. Jeff's up on his research, and he knows 80 percent of traditional mass-market cigars are bought by 45- to 65-year-old white males. His customer base, however, is 85 percent between the ages of twenty-eight and forty-five, and 20 percent of his clientele is female, compared to the mass market's 5 percent.

A mass-market customer might buy a whole box of cigars, Jeff points out. "That's twenty cigars of the exact same thing, which means they have the exact same experience twenty times, whereas our core customer wants to browse. They want different experiences. They want to come across different flavors," he says.

Now comes the fascinating synergy that happens when work and passion combine. Jeff clearly has a deep passion for his business: He loves cigars, he loves technology, and he has created a place where they meet. But remember—boutique products tend to be created by companies run with passion. Enter the boutique cigar manufacturer, which is a real thing. Jeff says there are even American tobacco fields dedicated to small-batch, limited-edition cigars, and that's not even counting the entrepreneurial, small-batch imports.

Mass-produced cigars tend to advertise traditionally: print and direct mail, complete with photographs of dark rooms filled with brown leather furniture. The boutique producer doesn't have the budget and, besides, their target customer would never see such an ad. Recall that the boutique producer sells cigars as an experience, not a product.

Their target customers are open to experimentation and variety. In other words, CigarClub and boutique cigar-makers are a marriage made in business heaven. Makers of these artisan cigars now seek the club's service to reach their target audience, prospecting not only for customers but for the prized social media commentary happy younger consumers generate.

CigarClub's passion shows in how it does business. The monthly mailings are not simply tossed in a cardboard box and chucked into the mail. Those three or five cigars are sealed in a metal-lined black bag that keeps them fresh up to twelve months, includes matches and, for first-time customers, a cigar cutter of the style they have chosen. Then comes the lagniappe—that unexpected little bonus—which is often a chocolate or a coffee product. The final packaging is exquisite—Jeff is a packaging buff and had a YouTube channel on the unpacking of Apple products back when he was in high school.

"The unboxing experience is important for us. We hope it takes you four or five minutes to sort through everything," he said.

And there you have it, passion in a cigar. Cigars, and tobacco products in general, have become pariah products to many, but those of us who love the experience of an occasional fine cigar around a campfire with good story-tellers are grateful there's passion still coursing through the industry.

Case Study

IT'S A WONDERFUL SUMMER
FOR A MOONDANCE

SHOW TITLE: *Moondance Adventures: A Summer Camp for Youth that Teaches Lessons for Life*

RELEASE DATE: *August 12, 2019*

Let's visit Moondance Adventures, an unusual summer camp experience for teens that's the passion of Hayes Hitchens. Hayes stumbled on his passion fortuitously as a college freshman, but it took him about sixteen years to really get there.

Here's how he tells it: "A great-aunt had started a summer camp in Wisconsin back in 1918 and just loved it. It stayed in the family and in my freshman year at Alabama, they had a staff slot open in the summer camp. And I discovered there's something about working with kids, something about being outdoors."

Hayes got the working-with-kids part down pretty quick, spending his early career at a prestigious private school in Atlanta. But he still hankered for the outdoors part. And that opportunity came when he was thirty-five and a summer camp came on the market. He and his partners got a business plan together, they lined up financing, Hayes quit his job—and the camp owners sold to someone else.

Hayes and his partners decided to go ahead—without the real estate. Moondance Adventures is headquartered in

Nashville, where Hayes and about ten other administrative employees are based; but the 110 young camp leaders set out for destinations that include Jackson Hole, Seattle and Anchorage in this country, with Costa Rica, Croatia, Geneva, Iceland, Norway and Tanzania among the international destinations. Some of the trips have service components built in, so kids might be working at a school in east Africa for part of the camp before setting out to climb Mount Kilimanjaro.

"We have challenging programs. We want them to find out what it is like to be pushed, to be in a small group and learn how everyone can support one another. What we are teaching them is how to be comfortable while being uncomfortable," Hayes says.

The format parks the helicopter parent at home, puts the tight-knit friend clique aside (no more than two friends can travel together), and the cell phones out of the picture for the duration. So are watches—campers are now rising and setting with the sun. Whichever of the five continents on the schedule they are visiting, whether they are hiking a glacier in Scandinavia or learning to scuba dive in Fiji, the destination is anywhere but the teens' comfort zone.

"The trip really starts when they get to the airport—flying independently is a great lesson," Hayes says. "There are some very real fears for kids. Are they gonna like me? Can I make it from Concourse A to Concourse B? Everybody should experience being out of their comfort zone and discovering that Yes, I can do this."

The zeal Hayes displays when he talks about his camp makes you wonder what would have happened if that long-ago summer camp real estate purchase had actually gone through as planned. My guess is Hayes would have run one heck of a stationary summer camp . . . but it wouldn't have been Moondance. Closing in on thirty years in business, this passionate summer camp operator says his biggest regret is how he doesn't get to go along with his campers.

Case Study

WHAT'S LIGHTING YOU UP?

SHOW TITLE: *Author Stephen Cope Discusses Discovering the Great Work of Your Life*

RELEASE DATE: *October 11, 2021*

It's all well and good to admire those whose work touches their passion, but how do we harvest those benefits for ourselves? There's got to be something we learn from these passion-infused businesses that we can put to work in our own lives. And there is!

As I was struggling with the work/passion question for myself awhile back, I came across Stephen Cope's *The Great Work of Your Life: A Guide for the Journey to Your True Calling*. If you are wondering if your career path has really taken you to your passion, consider this book a roadmap. In 2021, I was honored to have Cope join me on my broadcast to talk about how people can find the work they can be passionate about.

"We have a misapprehension in this culture that you are supposed to have one career and follow it through to retirement," Cope says.

Cope talks about *dharma*, which he describes as a "great, many-layered Sanskrit word that means sacred calling or vocation, or true calling." One dharma might not last a lifetime, and a restless soul might then drive you to seek a second or a third dharma, successively or all at once.

"There are three different areas that are important hunting grounds for dharma," Cope says. "The first one is this: What is it that is lighting you up at this point in your life? That is, what are you fascinated by, what are you drawn to? This is a very visceral experience of attraction. It may be way outside the field that you've studied, or it may be completely intuitive. But when we are on the hunt for dharma, we have to really pay attention to these visceral attractions.

"The second one is a very different hunting ground: What is the duty that you feel called to most profoundly at this point in life? What is it in life that if you do not do, that you will have a profound sense of self-betrayal? This can be very different from what lights you up, but they can also overlap," he says.

"The third area that is very productive in dharma is challenges and difficulties. Very often, challenges and difficulties—illness, divorce, relationship problems—very often these have the seed that is calling you forward into your future . . . Difficult moments; we don't invite them in, but they can be very good for the soul," Stephen says.

I highly recommend Cope's book to anyone struggling with doubts arising from a lack of passion in their work, especially if that work is something you once loved and now have begun to doubt. After all, Stephen told me, "There is a cultural bias that we are meant to do one thing, but we have multiple callings."

Case Study

HALF PIPE OR WALL ART?

SHOW TITLE: *Bear Walker—Making High-End Skateboards Worthy of Riding or Hanging as Art*

RELEASE DATE: *March 15, 2020*

I saved Bear Walker and his custom skateboards for the final story of this chapter. Bear illustrates that you can be extremely passionate about your business without being obsessive.

Bear is an under-the-radar celebrity, famous in the skateboarding world for the design aspects of his skateboards. At Bear Walker Industries in Fairhope, Alabama, he designs and oversees production of high-end specialty skateboards. For a premium, he'll make one to order. A custom Bear Walker will set you back between $1,000 to $2,000 and take awhile too. The meticulous craftsman puts as much as thirty hours into a custom board and has been known to scrap one if he is not satisfied with it.

"You're not going to see my boards in the X Games, but I have had people tell me my boards are so beautiful they decided to start skating," Bear says.

The Clemson University grad says he has really developed a new niche, so he has no real competitors beyond budget. "These boards are esthetically pleasing—but they're also a great ride," he says.

His multi-layered maple boards are carved and/or hand-painted and feature patent-pending grip capabilities (in other words, no grip tape, which will mean something to a skate-boarder). And, because of his deep love of pop culture, many of his designs draw from sources like the NBA and Pokémon. Yep, Pokémon, that collectible card trading/training game that is all '90s nostalgia—except it never really went away.

"I was in a rough spot a few years ago. I'd had a really big collaboration fall through and I was in a really weird spot. I heard Pokémon was going to be at this licensing expo in Vegas, so I made Pokémon a custom Pikachu skateboard and gave it to them at the show. They loved it. About two months later, I started getting calls from them, and that led to an ongoing partnership that allows my company to grow," he says.

Skateboarders aren't all, or even mostly, aspiring pros. Most just want to ride for fun. "It's kinda OK for people to just cruise around," Bear says.

His demographic is aged eighteen to thirty-four. They probably learned on skateboards their parents bought them, and now they can afford a $200 to $350 production model. The designer estimates that fully half of his boards wind up displayed on a wall instead of the sidewalk.

"We have a good chunk of people who have bought every board I have ever sold, as far as our limited editions go," Bear says. "That's lots of wall space."

At the ripe old age of thirty-one (at the time of the interview), Bear had an exit plan, and it's one that I love. Once he's made his money and had some fun, he's open to the idea of selling the business and staying on as creative director. That way, he hands off the paperwork and the day-to-day business but continues doing what he loves to do.

That's what I mean by passion not becoming obsession. Bear Walker loves his work and his skateboards—but they are not going to be the great white whale that eats the rest of his life.

So, oysters, cigars, summer camps, skateboards—all can be objects of passion, and that passion can drive your work life into your calling. I hope these entrepreneurs' stories have inspired you to keep searching for *your* next passion. It's out there.

⟶

WHAT WORKS

→ Personal passion drives small businesses focused on high quality.

→ Deep engagement and fulfillment in our work makes sustainable success more likely.

→ Your personal passion may be a potential profession—explore the possibilities.

→ Our professions—even the ones we stumble into—can turn out to be our passions, even if that wasn't the case at the beginning.

→ If you are fiercely passionate about a product or a service, you can find a clientele whose passion matches yours.

2

FIND A NICHE

A small but devoted clientele can fuel a great business.

American business has a fascinating phenomenon: the niche. Entrepreneurs find a narrow little space in the market—and they stay there. The business itself may grow, such as selling in five or twenty-five states instead of one or two, and it may become quite prosperous in the process, but the focus remains lasered-in on that niche. The niche business isn't trying to be all things to all people. Instead, it is one thing to some people. Do that well enough and you have a living. Do it exceptionally well, and you have a family business to pass along. Do it exceptionally well for long enough, and you have a legacy.

I love interviewing niche businesspeople on my radio program. Massive businesses sometimes roll along under their own weight, but those dealing in razor-thin slices of the market demand intense, hands-on direction from the helm. The people who are capable of running these sharply bordered businesses tend to be smart, decisive people. And, although I cannot tell you why this is, they also tend to be world-class storytellers. Maybe it's because they have to know every little nook and cranny of their niche, and the good stories are in those nooks and crannies.

Looking over my growing collection of interviews with niche business owners, I find entrepreneurs as diverse as the man who writes the final word on elevators all around the world, hardwood importers who travel the globe looking for lumber, a lawyer who branched out to make dog treats out of an invasive swamp rodent, and contractors who are catering to a new breed of homeowner with their "barndomeniums."

Case Study

YOUR NICHE OR MINE?

SHOW TITLE: *T. Bruce MacKinnon Teaches Us How to Dominate a Niche Market*

RELEASE DATE: *October 18, 2021*

Elevator World magazine dominates its niche. The first, and only, global magazine devoted to the elevator and "vertical transportation" industry has a worldwide circulation of ten thousand and runs a global operation—four employees at its Istanbul office, and another office in Bangalore, India—out of its Mobile, Alabama headquarters.

T. Bruce MacKinnon got into the business more than twenty years ago with his mother, who had joined her father in its launch. And T.—as he likes to be called—doesn't see anyone moving into *Elevator World's* particular niche. "I can't imagine even a huge publisher coming along to compete with us," he says—the family simply got into the niche too early, too thoroughly and does too good a job to leave room for competitors.

Elevator World is not just the magazine—it has regional publications in India, Turkey, Middle East, United Kingdom and Europe, a strategic partnership that takes it into South America, an annual directory, twelve newsletters and an entire education division. And keeping all that under control calls for a fair amount of globetrotting from T. and his mom.

"I think to dominate any business or any market, you've got to build relationships in the market," T. says.

Now, unless you are a contractor or at least building an ultra-high-end home, chances are you are unlikely to be in the market for an elevator, even though you may use one at the office every day. In these cases, I can't help but be curious: What's the price tag associated with this everyday item that I will never buy? While I had T. on the program, I had to ask him what an elevator for a four- or five-story office building would cost, say if you went with the "B-plus" version of the good stuff without going to the extreme? His answer, amongst all kind of variables, was in the neighborhood of $50,000 to $65,000 for a single elevator.

The industry uses "vertical transportation" as a more inclusive term than "elevators," to include escalators and "people-movers." A quick visit to *Elevator World's* website—and it will be a quick visit, because there's a paywall—shows elaborate projects taking shape in China, including those associated with the Winter 2022 Olympics, as well as an elegant private residential project in Dubai and a residential car garage in Canada.

The word "niche" may imply small, but even a very small part of a large thing is itself large. T. argues that niche industries are not marginalized, they're just overlooked.

"Don't think what you are doing doesn't matter, because it matters. I used to think the elevator industry was just the corniest thing ever, but it's literally a secret industry with phenomenal people, and I'm sure there's a number of other industries out there like that, so invest in it and see where it takes you," T. says.

Case Study

TIMBERRRRR!!!

SHOW TITLE: *A Niche Business Importing Exotic Timber for Specialized Uses—the Overseas Hardwoods Company*

RELEASE DATE: *May 20, 2019*

Luckett Robinson is one of four siblings involved in Overseas Hardwoods Company, headquartered in Mobile,

Alabama. Talk with him any length of time about his business, and you'll come away with a few new vocabulary words: ipe, zebrawood, merbau, and his favorite, apitong, also known as keruing. Not surprisingly, they're all types of trees, specifically trees that can be turned into lumber and sold in the U.S. marketplace.

"Apitong, that's a tough, durable wood that's been our bread and butter from the start," Luckett says.

How can a wood none of us have ever heard of previously be the foundation product for a successful company? Well, you would have heard of it if you were involved in transportation, because apitong is a natural product that performs well as flatbed trailer flooring. That sounds mundane until you think how many tractor-trailers you saw the last time you were on the highway.

"We make most of the flatbed trailer flooring that is wood," Luckett says. "Most of the U.S. military trailers use our wood floors."

Luckett's children are too young to be involved with the business yet, but they're already keenly aware of the family firm's go-to product, he said. When driving down the interstate on a family trip, those kids are checking out every passing flatbed or tractor-trailer with an open door, looking for their apitong.

Apitong is imported from Southeast Asia. Google the word and one of the first things you'll find on some websites is that it is considered endangered. The question had to be asked early in our encounter: Is this Mobile-based firm the one that is clearing the rainforests and killing the planet in the process?

"I would be the first to say responsible lumbermen are the biggest environmentalists you will find. We support sustainable harvesting because our livelihoods depend on it," Luckett says.

So, how do you make sure you are a responsible lumberman?

First of all, he says, pay attention to the country you are doing business in. Some have excellent records on responsible forest management—he named Malaysia among this group. Others haven't gotten there yet.

But the real secret to doing it right is the reason he and his brothers spend about 25 percent of their workdays traveling in Africa, Asia, Europe and South America.

"There's a difference between good responsible lumber folks and those that aren't, and it starts with visiting the supplier, who is harvesting timber legally and doing it the right way. The bulk of international purchasing is handled by the three brothers, and we try to visit core suppliers at least once a year or every other year: Malaysia, Indonesia, Burma, Africa, annually," Luckett says.

This is not tourism disguised as business travel. Friends who travel to Brazil on vacation talk about Rio de Janeiro, but the Robinsons aren't spending time in the cities. "I don't go to Rio, I go to mill towns in the middle of nowhere in Brazil. That's where you see things happening and that's where you can learn the quality of your supplier," he says.

"We don't tend to go to the places others visit. It's important to see if there's cars in the parking lot, trees in the mills."

And if they don't like what they see? He, his brothers and those who work for them walk away.

Funny thing, but concerns about lumber supplies critically shaped the development of the present company. When the family first got into lumber just over a hundred years ago, the current generation's grandfather and his brother started out with a sawmill, working regional timber. When the brother died prematurely, that business was sold off, but the family was into lumber to stay. In 1967, this generation's father started Overseas Hardwoods Company. He worked Europe, buying and selling, and became concerned that the housing boom driven by the Baby Boom would deplete America's supply of domestic oak. That concern drove his interest in imported lumber.

Importers operate in a highly regulated world, exposed to shifting tariffs and intense scrutiny. U.S. Customs and Border Patrol are concerned that invasive insect species might hitch a ride on imported lumber. For example, a shipment of lumber was quarantined at Savannah's port while a roach discovered among it was shipped off to the Smithsonian Institute to determine what kind it was, he said. Another example? A line of marching ants coming down a tow rope on a barge sparked inspectors' concerns, until a matching line of ants was discovered climbing up an adjoining rope. Seems the fire ants—yes, an invasive species but one that arrived over one hundred years ago—were merely touring the barge.

(Make a mental note of the modern precautions against importing invasive species. The subject, and its unforeseen and expensive consequences, will come up again a little later in this chapter.)

How is a family business big enough to peacefully accommodate four siblings? There's Lee Robinson, president of the firm. Gregory is the vice president of operations, and Luckett—a self-described "recovering lawyer"—handles finance and serves as general counsel. Sister, Therese Hillyer, handles the administrative side of the business. In all, the company employs about 190 people across operations in Alabama, California, Texas, Washington and Wisconsin.

Luckett credits the siblings' upbringing—especially the influence of their mother, who reared a brood of eight with the mantra of getting along.

"I tell people a family business can be the absolute best business in the world, and it can also be the worst business," Luckett says. "We all grew up being respectful of one another. But you have to work hard. The willingness to work long and hard is critical. We work through issues and reach consensus on the best way to go."

Apitong, that workhorse wood that floors much of America's flatbed trailer fleet, may be the bread and butter of the Robinsons' business, but Overseas Hardwoods also has its share of high-profile, name-dropper projects—from the specialty teak used by Viking Yachts, to the Ipe (an extremely durable Brazilian hardwood Luckett calls "the Lamborghini of decking products) used in the Atlanta Braves' Truist Park.

26

Case Study

NUTRIA-ISHOUS

SHOW TITLE: *Turning Invasive Nutria into Dog Food—The Fantastic Story of Marsh Dog Pet Treats*

RELEASE DATE: *October 10, 2020*

You have to be a pretty savvy entrepreneur to find a business opportunity embedded in wetlands overrun with nutrias, an invasive South American rodent. That's just what Hansel Harlan, founder of Marsh Dog Pet Treats, did. And the tale of how he did it is too weird and too funny to be anything but true.

First of all, what's a nutria? It's a South American critter whose fertility and appetite are severely damaging to wetlands, where they feast on the roots of marsh vegetation. They are problems in several coastal states—I can even remember blasting away at them in the Mobile Delta on boyhood hunting trips—but Louisiana has a particularly bad case of them. The animals look like a cross between a rat and a beaver, with orangish buck teeth and webbed hind feet. (If that description does not drive you to Google to look at a photograph, you were born without natural curiosity.)

The animals were originally brought to this country for their fur, and it didn't take long for them to escape and establish wild populations in areas to which they were well suited. When the fur industry was flourishing, hunters kept the population in some sort of balance. Then, about the mid-'80s, the fur market virtually disappeared—and the wild nutria population exploded.

State and federal governments soon realized they had a problem on their hands. (And now that story of sending a roach off for identification while a load of lumber was quarantined makes a lot more sense, doesn't it?) A mass poisoning program was considered but rejected, since it would kill off native wildlife as well.

Next up was a state of Louisiana plan to market nutria meat as a delicacy, as it is treated in South America. "The meat is pretty good, sort of like squirrel. It doesn't have a lot of taste, until you mix it with a sauce piquant," Hansel says.

That plan faced an uphill climb, largely because the animals—let's be frank here—look like giant rats. It didn't help, Hansel adds, that at the same time as the eat-a-nutria campaign was going on, a high-profile gung-ho parish sheriff led his deputies on highly publicized nighttime hunting expeditions to kill nutria "rats" in the area.

Eventually, Louisiana fell back on a classic bounty program that still goes on today. Get a permit, get assigned a territory, and the state of Louisiana will pay you $6 for every nutria tail you turn in during the November-March season. (The season is limited because the program depends on trapping, which doesn't discriminate among species.)

So, how did Hansel get involved with nutria? It's kind of hard to picture a Baton Rouge attorney slogging through the marsh blasting away at nuisance animals for $6 a pop. And that's not what happened. Instead, his dog led him to the nutria program. Seems the family dog suffered from allergies, and Hansel found himself cooking dog food at home out of brown rice and turkey. Then, during the "nutria as food" campaign, he read an article that compared the meat to turkey—and wheels started to turn when he learned of a combined state and federal program seeking to address the problems of the Barataria-Terrebonne National Estuary. He got together with his sister to discuss possibilities.

"We said, 'Why don't we fill out a grant application and tell them we want to make dog treats out of nutria and see what happens?' So we did. And the next thing you know, they said 'Congratulations, you won, here's $15,000. When are you going to start?' So we said, 'Oh, shoot, when are we going to start?'" Hansel recalls.

Now, they really weren't as clueless as that. The Harlans had some family connection to the Barq's Rootbeer operation (now part of Coca-Cola), so there were relatives to turn to who were familiar with food processing and marketing. They just superimposed nutria processing onto that basic business plan, located a processor who would actually convert nutria carcasses into varieties of soft or crunchy dog treats, and they were in business. Nor did any member of the family have to suit up to hunt nutria, because the company turned to aggregators who bought the carcasses from the bounty hunters. Marsh Dog Treats even became a national media darling, because what reporter could resist a story about solving an ecological problem by feeding it to your dog?

Does that mean Louisiana has solved its nutria problem? After all, the founder says the company's unofficial motto is "Put us out of business."

"The problem is, the problem doesn't go away. What the nutria control program does is mow the grass each year, year after year. You have to harvest four hundred thousand nutria per year in Louisiana just to keep the population stable," Hansel says.

For the record, Chasing Our Tails, a Minnesota manufacturer of dog treats and chews, has acquired Marsh Dog since Hansel and I spoke in the fall of 2020. The treats are still being produced from wild Louisiana nutria and are available via the internet.

Case Study

NEW AGE BARN RAISING

SHOW TITLE: *Barndominiums—They're a Thing. A BIG Thing. John Quinnelly Builds a Bunch of Them.*

RELEASE DATE: *July 20, 2020*

Who knew there were still niches to be discovered and exploited in the homebuilding industry? Certainly not me—at least not until I was introduced to John Quinnelly and Allen Ivy of Valor Steel Buildings, based in Daphne, Alabama, and Gary Gordon of Gordon Construction, which serves as Valor's interior construction arm. The three of them got together to talk with me about a phenomenon that has quickly mushroomed into a major part of their business—barndominiums.

What's a barndominium? It's a steel structure that incorporates multiple uses—storage, workspace, and living quarters—under a single roof. The steel building can be dressed up to resemble a conventional house more closely. Or not, as the case may be.

"Barndominiums are something that originated out of Texas. Basically, what it is, people have a lot of toys—RVs, boats and trucks—and they want all of those things in one spot, and they want to have their house in the same spot. So combining all those things in one structure is what it's about," says John.

Think about a typical, affluent suburbanite. Maybe the second car is parked in the driveway because the jet skis are taking up space in the garage. The homeowners' association won't let this guy work on his hot rod in the driveway, so he's renting space at a garage or racetrack. The family has to pay to store their RV offsite, and it has to be fetched to begin preparation for any trip. Or maybe the wife is into horses, and they're stabled elsewhere. All this expensive stuff they bought to have fun with is running up rental fees and out of immediate reach. No wonder the idea of corralling all that under one roof appeals—especially with highly flexible open-plan interiors.

Allen says 40 percent of their firm's work is now on barndominiums, along with the conventional steel buildings for businesses, industry and even churches. It's an idea that has caught on fast.

Where are these things going up? "More in the outskirts, in more rural areas, maybe where building permits and covenants are not as stringent," Allen says. "They do look like a metal building but we can put aesthetics on it, bricks or siding to give it a residential feel."

In other words, maybe the idea of what a home is is changing. After all, Gary points out, lots of people, especially retirees, are buying RVs and just living in them. A barndominium, with interior storage space for that RV, combines conventional living space with storage, and the homeowner can even use the RV as a guest room or, depending on its size, a guest apartment.

"You have no load-bearing walls, so if we build you a 40-foot, 50-foot, 60-foot-wide building, you can have any size room you like," says John.

An added appeal, the three builders agree, is that a barndomium can be built for about 30 percent less than a conventional house of the same size. None of the ones he has participated in have come back on the market yet, Gary notes, so getting comps for real estate sales is sort of an open-ended question.

What's the biggest selling point, though?

"The functionality," Gary says. "[People] have no idea, they can have what they want as living quarters. One lady wants to put four stalls for horses and a wash area and a space between that, and then the living quarters, all under one roof—and we can do that."

These guys can talk convincingly about the hurricane-resistant, termite-starving qualities of their unconventional structures, as well as amenities like wraparound porches, fireplaces, and interior detailing that cannot be distinguished from conventional homes.

But to me, the most amazing thing about barndominiums is that they exist at all. The American housing market is an evolving thing, forever adapting and changing. Today's McMansions, those giant two-story houses packed onto lots with minimal yard space, will one day look as dated as our grandparents' clapboard bungalows. I guess I knew on some level that the house my children choose to live in one day will differ radically from my own hard-won house. But somehow, I never envisioned the guest room for their visiting parents might be an RV.

So, we've looked at four very different niche businesses—an international specialty publication focused solely on elevators, exotic imported hardwoods, dog treats that repurpose problem animals as protein, and a new type of housing that might redefine what home means to lots of folks. What lessons can we draw from this wild variety of innovation in very narrow spaces?

For one thing, a good idea is a good idea, even if occupies an extremely small niche. In the competitive world of dog treats, there's a high-end tier for folks who are as careful about what they feed their dog as they are about what they feed their other children, and that's the tier Marsh Dog Treats aimed at. And their ecological strength helped them carve out a slice of that market.

For another thing, operating in a tightly defined niche doesn't excuse you from intense management requirements.

In fact, it amplifies them. Your kids cannot inherit your lumber business if there are no trees to harvest, and a high-end clientele for exotic woods doesn't want the onus of environmental predation on their latest remodel, so companies like Overseas Hardwoods Company are checking up on their suppliers in person, even in the back of beyond.

And finally, today's niche product may dominate the mainstream in the future. Who knows, we may all be sharing a roof with our boat and our RV twenty years from now.

WHAT WORKS

→ If a product or service appeals to a small but devoted clientele, it can be a sustainably successful business.

→ A niche can be based on a specialized need, or a widely used product but with a special story attached.

→ Changes in lifestyle, technology, and ways of life constantly create new niches to serve.

→ Niches generally have less competition than broader-based products and services.

→ Current communication technology makes it easier than ever for niche businesses to find their customers, and vice versa.

3

INNOVATE

Look beyond time-honored ways to break through in the marketplace.

*S*ome rules were meant to be broken, and I can prove this with baseball and bacon.

This is not a blanket endorsement of anarchy. Most rules exist for one reason and one reason only—they work, and time has proven that they work. But those same rules with a proven track record of success can become an obstacle to progress when they don't keep up with the times, the technology and the trends of the modern business world.

I found two sterling examples of constructive rule-breaking—let's call it *innovation*—among my crop of interview subjects, and I know I could have found lots more had I kept looking. These two entrepreneurs—one in baseball, one in bacon—took on systems entrenched in history and tradition and succeeded. They knew there was a better way and they busted through. Let's look at how they did it and see if similar innovation might get your business moving in a profitable, if unexpected, direction.

Case Study

STRIKE THREE OR HOME RUN?

SHOW TITLE: *Adam Heisler Teaches Non-Traditional Baseball Skills in a City Steeped in Baseball Tradition*

RELEASE DATE: *February 8, 2021*

Let's start with baseball because, well, I love baseball. More than any other sport, there are stories attached to baseball, and Adam Heisler's story is a particularly good one. No, he's not going to be inducted at Cooperstown, at least not as a player, but he made a good living playing the game he loves and has found a way to bring that career back to his hometown of Mobile. And all of this despite having said "No" to baseball's draft—twice!—early in his career.

One of the things I love about baseball is it has a life outside the giant machine of the modern-day Major League Baseball. Mobile may have lost its minor league team as part of the "Build me a fancy new stadium or I'll take my team and move" movement, but what the city can never lose is its storied baseball tradition. Mobile has been the home of five Baseball Hall of Famers, and yes, you read that right. (And just to save any curious readers the trouble of looking it up, that set of five consists of Hank Aaron, Willie McCovey, Satchel Paige, Ozzie Smith and Billy Williams—as impressive a bunch of hometown heroes as anyone could ask for.)

Now Mobile, by and large, is a city that embraces tradition, and baseball itself is literally steeped in tradition. So it stands to reason that Mobile baseball is even *more* tradition-oriented than baseball elsewhere. Yet into this stately environment, a few years ago, came a former baseball pro who proceeded to shake up the way youngsters—and even the occasional pro seeking to polish his skills—learn the game.

"I was drafted out of high school. I was a seventeen-year-old, and I wasn't ready to go out on my own. Even I knew that. For one thing, I was on the smaller side, even though I was really fast," remembers Adam. So, he opted to go to junior college and continue playing, and growing up. He moved on to a senior college and again turned the draft down in his junior year—a move he later regretted when he suffered an injury during his senior year.

But he did ultimately make it into the pro ranks, playing outfield for farm teams for the Chicago White Sox for four years and another two years in Winnipeg, Canada. When his playing options were narrowed down to Mexico, he decided to come home to Mobile and get into private coaching by setting up the Heisler Heat Baseball Academy.

So far, none of this sounds like rule-breaking, does it? Unless you overlook saying "no" twice to an MLB draft. But the academy Adam set up was more than just the "practice, practice, practice" extension of school teams and travel ball for aspiring tweens and teens. Instead, Adam brought to Mobile the technology that adds a scientific edge to player development. With that new equipment came a new vocabulary, phrases like "launch angle," "exit velocity," "bat speed" and "angle of attack."

Video technology that can analyze a swing in a batting cage and tell the hitter and his coach where that particular ball would have gone on the field, and at what angle and speed, is readily available for those who have deep-enough pockets. Surprisingly, though, Adam says, it hasn't been welcomed with open arms by baseball's coaching community, at least among those who work with young players.

"The launch angle—when you speak about it to players or coaches who don't understand it, it's almost like you said a swear word. They look at you with big eyes, like 'I can't believe you just mentioned launch angle,'" says Adam. "It's just a metric for how the ball hits the bat."

"Launch angle" is actually a physics term, and the new technology in baseball is adding a layer of precision based in physics to player development. Using tools like the Rapsodo Hitting Monitor bridges "old school" and "new school" baseball, Adam says.

While pro coaches may feel differently, Adam knows that high school coaches may be uncomfortable with the technology-driven approach to player development. Accordingly, he says, he advises the boys he coaches to keep mum about the new vocabulary and new technique.

"When they leave our facility, I tell them not to talk about their swing: Their coach may get offended by that. Our rule is don't even mention it outside, don't even talk about it. It'll backfire. The coach writes the lineup, I do not," Adam says.

Golf, unlike baseball, has wholeheartedly embraced what technology can do in analyzing a swing, he acknowledges. But you don't have to have the thousands of dollars to invest in the equipment to benefit from technology, he says: Just have someone video the player's swing on a cell phone to see where body mechanics might be going wrong. There are even apps where you can look at live pitches and train to recognize what kind of pitch is thrown and if it is a strike or not. And the old basics remain the same, too, he adds—years of developing hand-eye coordination before moving on to how to move the body.

With the help of technology-assisted player development, Adam says he's seen twelve-year-olds hitting home runs. "I didn't get my first home run until high school," he says.

So, with all this science coming to bear on the basic at-bat, are we in for an era where batting averages climb, and hitting .350, .400 isn't that impressive?

Adam laughs that one off, asking "Have you seen what pitchers are throwing these days?"

So, Adam risks the wrath of school-level coaches to put technology to work for his students. And who are those students? Anyone from Little Leaguers on up whose parents can pay the freight. As of this writing, a semi-private lesson with Adam or one of his academy's other coaches runs $60, after an initial session priced at twice that. The academy (heislerheatbaseball.com) also offers multi-day camps during school breaks.

How does Adam measure the success of his efforts? Is he waiting to see which of the players he brought along from childhood breaks into the majors?

"I think success is continuing to pass down knowledge. I visit facilities, and I do a podcast with my buddy in Indiana. I want to pass down this knowledge, serve these kids and help them reach their ultimate potential," he says. "The coolest stuff is if a kid who used to bat tenth now bats fourth or third and is one of the better players on his team."

And that's worth breaking a few rules for!

Case Study

THAT'LL DO, PIG!! THAT'LL DO!!!

SHOW TITLE: *Bill E. Stitt Makes the World's Best Bacon in Fairhope, Alabama*

RELEASE DATE: *May 3, 2021*

Well, let's move from the tradition-bound world of baseball to that of bacon, small-batch, high-end bacon. How can you break the rules in bacon? Do rules even *exist* in bacon?

The answer is yes, they do, and they center around the conventional way of preserving pork bellies as bacon. Slowing down and taking a distinctive and less processed way of making bacon? Yep, that's definitely breaking, if not rules, at least some conventions. (And let me hastily add here, the bacon we're talking about is produced under USDA regulations and standards: There are certain rules you *don't* break when you are producing food for human consumption.)

But before I go on to tell you about Bill E. Stitt and his Bill-E's Small Batch Bacon, let's pause to talk about how trendy bacon currently is and just what "trendy" means.

As you know, I spend a large part of my professional life on the speakers' circuit, addressing audiences amassed from major companies and trade organizations. This life affords me an excellent opportunity to meet and learn from other experts on that same circuit. David Zach, a futurist, is one of those experts who not only speaks but writes. He's worth the read, or the listen if your paths ever cross.

One of the things David talks about (and much more eloquently than I can) is the difference between fads, trends and principles. Fads are the passing fancies of the day, very short-lived. It's hard to make business hay out of fads, to get in while they're hot and out as they cool, and so David advises they are best left ignored. Trends, on the other hand, last longer and are influential; businesses must react to them. I'll pull an example from my own professional life: Whereas most of us on the speakers' circuit work to keep an audience seated and engaged for in the neighborhood of an hour, the TED Talk came along with its shorter, YouTube-friendly monologues. With more than 3,500 TED Talks available free on YouTube today, the format clearly is something much more lasting than a fad. Speakers now have to step into that format with the same impact as far longer presentations. And just to close the loop on the three things David contrasts and compares, principles are unchanging and don't come and go. Examples include customer service, sound financial management, and honesty and integrity.

But how can bacon be a trend? After all, people have been eating bacon since, well, since they met pigs. It's nothing new.

But surely you have noticed that bacon isn't just for breakfast anymore. We have specialty bacons and bacon jam and even chocolate bacon. You'll find bacon festivals all across the country, seemingly every place that has a convention and visitors bureau to stage them. Archie McPhee, a novelty store mainly based on the internet, sells bandage strips shaped like bacon, bacon-scented candles and a scarf patterned like uncooked bacon. Etsy offers bacon-scented wrapping paper, at least eight different models of bacon earrings and, yes, real bacon.

Now, the sillier-sounding products—by which I mean those you cannot eat—would mean bacon is having a fad moment. But the festivals, the serious attention from chefs, the plethora of boutique bacons? That, my friends, is a trend—and long may it trend, because I love me some bacon.

Bill E. identified as a foodie when he was a teenager in Yazoo City, Mississippi, but he didn't get a chance to exercise his passion for bacon until his student days at Ole Miss. Everybody knows college students will eat anything, and Bill E.'s college friends got to eat his bacon experiments. It didn't take him too long to hit on what he considers perfection.

"It's a lifelong endeavor," is how Bill E. puts it. "I wanted to be as natural and pure and traditional as possible. The original goal was to produce bacon the way our ancestors did. It's heavy salt, brown sugar, real molasses, it's a timing and a temperature thing. And then you've got to sing to it."

You heard that right—sing to it. There's a stage at his restaurant in Fairhope, Alabama, where folks are encouraged to sing to the bacon in the adjacent USDA-approved processing facility (and Bill E. thinks Mississippi Delta blues work best). It's there that the bacon is cured for eight days before moving on to the hickory smoking process.

The result is a phenomenal bacon that you can buy in the Piggly Wiggly grocery stores in south Alabama and on Rodeo Drive in Beverly Hills and a couple of places in Manhattan. And, of course, there's the internet, where two pounds of Bill-E's Small Batch Bacon will set you back $49.95. (I can't speak for the prices on Rodeo Drive, but when I pick it up at the Piggly Wiggly for my own table, it's in the neighborhood of $12.99 per package.)

"My raw ingredients cost more," Bill E. says by way of explanation. So maybe this isn't the bacon you fix when all the cousins' kids are at the beach house. Instead, fix them conventional bacon and send them off happy, then break out the "adult" bacon, he suggests.

Bill E. started breaking the rules with his packaging, right off the bat. "My wrapper doesn't have a window. So many butchers told me it would never sell because it doesn't have a window," he says.

He also breaks the rules by encouraging grocers to keep his product out of the regular bacon section. "Put it next to the steaks, the porterhouses. When they bury it in the bacon, it does OK, but when they put it next to the steaks, it just blows up," he says.

Bill E. wishes he could locally source the pork bellies his operation consumes, but the specs he sets and the volume he requires make that impossible. He chooses Berkshire Reds and Chantilly Whites as his meat source—breeds that, as he puts it, "are not designer pigs that've been manipulated a bunch; it's a true breed that has been around for centuries." He wants them raised humanely and with other standards as well. So he's working with twenty-five small farms (up from the original three) in southern Iowa and Illinois, where he buys all the pork bellies they raise. He thinks it is important to know where the meat comes from, both for producers and consumers.

"The largest pork producer in the U.S. was bought by the Chinese. I'm not anti-anyone, but a lot of people want to buy American," Bill says.

Thinking about rule breaking, I asked him about using feral hogs as a meat source. The invasive species is a damaging nuisance in multiple states, and making it into tasty bacon would help solve the problem. But that's a non-starter for Bill E. As much as wild hogs need to be eradicated, they lack the uniform flavor needed to produce a commercial product. "You can bring me six hogs from one hunt, and they'd all taste completely different," he says.

How long do food trends last? I asked Bill E., a veteran restaurateur in addition to being a bacon producer. "Bacon is always going to be here," he says, "and I think there's a place for chocolate bacon."

His restaurant offers a Bill-E's Chocolate Belly, described as a combination of bacon and salted caramel brownie bites covered with bourbon brown sugar glaze and a smoked cherry.

Bill E. says he never doubted he would achieve bacon Nirvana. "I had a little smoker and I was always process oriented," he says. "The first and second times were trial and error, but by the third time I made it as a college student, I knew there would be a time when I would explode with this."

What goals does he have for the future, since the bacon needs no further work (as my household can attest)? If he had more space, he says, he'd like to process whole hogs instead of the trimmed pork bellies he now handles. His experiments with using his method on pork shoulders, hams and ribs always sell out at the restaurant, he notes. Speaking of the restaurant, he'd like to expand the restaurant idea too. But most of all, he wants his bacon to be in the great restaurants across the country.

"I am having so much fun. We've got a long way to go, and we need more people, but we're going to get there," Bill E. says.

What can we, as business leaders, take away from these examples of baseball and bacon? For one thing, they tell us that even the most hidebound of traditions, both large and small, should be reexamined every now and then. Embracing the future, like Adam with his technology-driven player development, and rediscovering the past, like Bill E. with his heritage breed hogs and simple ingredients, may take us out of our comfort zone and into more profitable places.

———➤

WHAT WORKS

- → If it's "always been done that way," it's probably time to explore other ways.

- → Ever-changing technology constantly offers new ways to evaluate and improve the way we do things.

- → If a product is already great, that doesn't mean there's not a way to make it better.

- → Innovation often meets resistance. That doesn't mean it's wrong.

- → In mature markets, innovation may be the only way to create new opportunities.

4

BE PERSISTENT

Push past the gauntlet
of "no" to get to "yes."

What can a $15 milkshake, a doctor who treats only uninsured patients, and a gifted singer with a long-deferred dream teach us about business? The value of *persistence*. If you're going to start a business and keep it going, you're going to have to blow right past a lot of "No thanks." Not every door will open immediately, and the first folks you make your pitch to might shrug. But you need to keep going until you get a "Yes," even a small one. That's when you get your chance. Let's meet some folks who've walked that never-give-up walk and see where it's taken them.

Case Study

DRIP. TRICKLE. GUSH!

SHOW TITLE: *Marquis Forge Heard the Call. Obeyed. And Is Now Selling LOTS of Water.*
RELEASE DATE: *April 1, 2019*

SHOW TITLE: *Eleven86 Water—Another Conversation with the Incredible Marquis Forge*
RELEASE DATE: *October 20, 2019*

Marquis Forge is a good starting point. He could teach us all a lesson in never giving up. When he was trying to get his artesian water bottling operation off the ground, he applied to eighteen banks for a business loan—and was turned down eighteen times. Yet today, Eleven86 Water is off and running and has even been named the official water of the state of Alabama. If he had given up after collecting his eighteenth rejection, his midlife business venture would never have sold a single bottle—and Marquis' hometown of Autaugaville, Alabama, would be the poorer for it.

Let's revisit those rejections with the banks. Have you ever applied for a business loan? Other than medical procedures or an IRS audit, there's nothing more invasive, stressful or disheartening. Each of those eighteen banks probably had a slightly different application process, just enough so that you had to do the whole thing over again to satisfy them. That's eighteen spaced-out appointments to prepare for, including sleepless nights beforehand and a tightening in your gut as you walk into a banker's plush office. And the decisions wouldn't have been immediate, either—at least some of those banks would have kept you waiting. Furthermore, in Marquis' case, a few of the banks had something worse than "No" to say.

"I'm talking about eighteen banks looking at our business plan, telling us we were crazy, telling us nobody in Alabama is going to buy bottled water. One banker told us if you came to us with the five worst business plans, five business models, we would choose them ten times before we chose you," he remembers.

After eighteen soul-draining attempts, no one would have blamed Marquis if he had given up. In fact, most of us would have given up well before that. Those eighteen tries convinced Marquis that the banks were a dead end for him, at least for the moment. But that's where the application of a "Never Give Up!" philosophy takes over. Marquis kept trying—but he changed his tactic. Instead of collecting additional rejections from banks, he turned to his own resources and began liquidating things for cash, and so did his family and friends.

"We dug the well out of our pocket; we bought the land out of our pocket; we dug the building foundation out of our pocket; we put the building up out of our pocket," he said.

And just when those pockets started to run dry, along came a state business development grant. And right behind that was a phone call—from a nineteenth bank. Eleven86 Water closed on a loan four months later. The water, along with the financial resources, has flowed continuously since then—all because Marquis and his team understood that never giving up was more than repeating what hadn't worked before. It included finding a new approach and continuing to try.

Now, Eleven86 Water had assets going for it, among them the incredibly pure artesian water that is its product. But it also has Marquis, who has been sort of the poster child for the never-give-up movement since his teenage years. When he gave the valedictorian's speech at Autaugaville School, he vowed to never forget where he came from, and to return someday to benefit his hometown.

Marquis went off to the University of Alabama, where he earned a spot on the football team as a walk-on. Let that sink in: Here's a powerhouse collegiate football program with no shortage of money and talent, recruiting successfully across the country, and this teenage kid from a tiny town tries out—and makes the team. Now, this isn't a Hallmark Movie, so he didn't end his football career with a game-winning play in the Iron Bowl, but he was on the team and he got some playing time. In a state with a gloried football tradition like Alabama, having worn that uniform represented something, then and now.

Marquis had another advantage when he abruptly changed careers from the automotive industry. You see, Marquis is a man of faith, and he says he's in the water business because God told him to be. It's not business acumen or financial savvy, he says, but obedience that brought him to develop Autaugaville's natural resources. That's the kind of statement that won't impress a bank loan committee—i.e., those eighteen bank rejections. But it is a deep belief that shows you something about the man and explains his confidence and passion and dogged persistence.

Marquis had spent twenty years in Alabama's booming automobile industry before making his leap of faith into the water business. He was at a point in his career where I've noticed similar things about other businesspeople, including myself. We're looking down the road at our work life's home stretch and we're wondering what the last fifteen, twenty years at the job are going to look like. A financially secure retirement and thinking of playing with as-yet-unborn grandchildren is nice, but many of us want something more—a legacy, a footprint, an impact.

Those thoughts were definitely in Marquis' mind when he began revisiting the promise he had made to his hometown when he was a high school senior. He'd promised to give back to his community, and that community needed his help.

Small towns across rural Alabama, actually across rural America as a whole, are struggling. Agricultural-based lifestyles are in decline. Towns have lost retail ground to larger cities and the internet. Children may still grow up in a town where everybody knows their name, but when they're grown, they're going to have to look elsewhere to earn a living. Increasingly, they must drive farther to find a job, to get groceries, even to buy gas.

Marquis sees Eleven86 Water as part of the solution for Autaugaville. His bottling plant involves a deep well that taps into the signature pure water in an underground aquifer. The company pumps it, gives it the minimal treatment required by law, and bottles it in plastic bottles that are blown on-site. The plant started out in 2018 with ten employees, and ultimately will employ more than twenty-five.

In your average American metropolis, ten jobs is not even a drop in the bucket. In Autaugaville, population 963 by a 2019 Census estimate, ten jobs (with the promise of more) matter. Marquis gets an evangelical zeal in his voice when he talks about employees who can walk to work or drive only one or two minutes versus long commutes, about employees who can reach their child's school in only a few minutes and don't lose their paid time off coping with a sick child.

"We want to help revitalize this town. We want a grocery store, we want a 24/7 convenience store, we want hotels, we want restaurants; we don't want anyone else to come and say the foot traffic is not enough," he says. In other words, he wants his hometown back, back as a functioning destination and not just a wide place on an over-traveled road. And he believes good jobs and a proud product will get Autaugaville there. Because, after all, he promised, all those years ago.

Case Study

TWO SCOOPS OF WORK WITH
SPRINKLES ON TOP

SHOW TITLE: *The Yard Milkshake Bar—Beautiful Treats, Huge Growth, and a* Shark Tank *Deal*

RELEASE DATE: *January 5, 2020*

Real estate is a major part in Chelsea and Logan Green's never-give-up story. These are the folks with the $15 milkshake. Not only do people not laugh at the thought of paying that for a fancy cup of calories, they line up to purchase it. But, again, it took them awhile to get there.

Both Chelsea and Logan grew up in entrepreneurial families in and around Gulf Shores, Alabama, and cut their teeth working in their parents' businesses. Things were rocking along and then, in 2010, disaster struck. The explosion and sinking of the oil rig Deepwater Horizon in the Gulf of Mexico led to the worst oil spill yet encountered in this country. Coastlines were contaminated from Texas to Florida, and right in the middle of that swath was the Alabama coast.

Environmental disasters are economic disasters as well, and soon people who didn't even make their living directly from the sea were feeling the impact. Chelsea's dad was one of them. A piece of property he owned was left vacant by an ice cream shop that didn't survive the hit tourism took in the wake of the oil spill. Rather than sit idle during the tourist season, Chelsea and her mom set up shop in it and Island Ice Cream was born. Chelsea still owns it.

And there things sat for several years. Turns out, Chelsea was pretty good at the ice cream business. So much so, that a property owner who had seen three frozen dessert shops fail in one of his storefronts came calling to see if Chelsea wanted to give it a go.

You saw the red warning flag buried in that last sentence, right? Three failures in the same location, all involving a similar product (one of them that nitrogen-frozen confection that was all the rage for a while)? We all know pieces of property like that—seemingly prime locations where restaurants or gift shops or whatever open with fanfare and die a quick death. When considering expanding your business, beware of property that is littered with husks of previous tenants.

But Chelsea wondered if that red flag was really a disguised opportunity. In this case, the never-give-up aspect was for the property itself, already three times a failure. What if, she wondered, she came up with something absolutely unique for that location? And the idea of a super-premium, tricked-out, high-quality milkshake was born.

"We wanted something no one in our area had ever seen. We wanted to use all these crazy toppings," Chelsea says. So, she began experimenting in Island Ice Cream and customers who watched her build the experimental milkshake creations tried to order them. That's when she knew she was onto something, and the first The Yard Milkshake Bar opened to a line of waiting customers that's pretty much there all summer long.

Now, bear in mind that a specialty milkshake from The Yard Milkshake Bar bears about as much resemblance to an ordinary fast-food concoction as a wedding cake does to a pancake. These are sculptural creations, starting with a high-butterfat specialty ice cream served in a keepsake pint jar with a rim dipped in coating, rolled in various treats, then piled high with toppings that range from a whole cupcake to an entire banana or a white chocolate depiction of a mermaid's tail.

The specialty shakes were not originally envisioned as the bread-and-butter of the brand. The menu includes many smaller, simpler and cheaper treats. Logan says, "We have $3 and $4 bowls and cones—but people don't really buy them."

So if it is perceived as valuable in its over-the-top form, yes, people will pay $15 for a milkshake because they are really buying more than a milkshake—they are buying a vacation experience shaped, more or less, like a milkshake.

At this point, the never-give-up portion of the story kicks back in. The concept caught on with a vengeance and the Greens soon had several The Yard Milkshake Bars. The concept called out for franchising—but franchising is a complicated process. Now, cue reality television.

Representatives of the ABC reality series *Shark Tank*, in which business tycoons hear business pitches and decide which applicants to support with investment, approached the couple. The Greens agreed to participate and spent six months honing their presentation. When they finally got their shot, they were offered a deal by the show's Mark Cuban.

Now, that handshake at the end of the show is really just the beginning of a deal and not the conclusion of one, the couple explained. After due diligence on both sides, the Greens decided not to go with Cuban's offer because they didn't want to give up controlling their franchise plans themselves.

"There's no amount of money you can throw at a business to make all your problems go away," Logan says. "You're not going to want to work on a problem, it's not going to be a good time, but to give away equity for that was going to be a bit irresponsible. When those problems go away and they're solved, you still own your company."

But the national television program led to publicity for the Greens, and it is still featured on their website. Meanwhile, they've mastered franchising on their own, and The Yard Milkshake Bar is now in Vancouver, Washington, Atlanta, and other locations in Louisiana, Mississippi, Virginia, Tennessee, Texas and Arizona. And the whole operation is still in the family's hands, because the Greens decided to figure out franchising on their own rather than trade equity for expertise. It's another example of never giving up, even to make things easier.

Case Study
BROKEN BODIES. BENDED KNEES

SHOW TITLE: *Victory Health Partner's Mission: Service Plus Excellent Healthcare*

RELEASE DATE: *October 19, 2020*

So far, we've drawn our examples from bottled artesian water and luxury milkshakes. But the next never-give-up example can be more of a life-and-death situation.

Dr. Robert Lightfoot is a general surgeon in the Mobile area, and he began to reevaluate his medical career as he and his wife were participating in a medical mission trip to Venezuela, bringing health care to people who "literally did not have two pennies to rub together," as he puts it. When he returned home, he discovered a calling to do something for the medically underserved in his own community.

He focused on the group most likely to fall through the cracks—low-income, uninsured adults between the ages of eighteen and sixty-five. Programs exist to help low-income children, he found, but not the working poor and others in similar places on the socio-economic ladder. "What usually falls out in the juggling of their budgets is their own medications," Lightfoot says. "One major hospitalization for this demographic could ruin them financially for the rest of their lives."

But there can't be a clinic without a building to house it. Lightfoot and the group of like-minded souls he'd gathered were offered two free buildings, but neither was the right fit. Then, along came just the right place—an 11,000-square-foot medical office building. "The price was $850,000 and we didn't have eight dollars and fifty cents," is Lightfoot's account.

The story could have ended there, but the team who would become Victory Health Partners was familiar with the never-give-up refrain. They spent the following two years working on their clinic-less project and, since Lightfoot calls his operation "blatantly Christian," praying for that home.

"It was a time of planning and preparation anyway," says the surgeon. "We knew we needed to persist, just doing the planning of it, just getting ready. We knew if we just persisted, well, a lot of times when you get to the point where you just think it's never going to happen, that's right when it IS going to happen."

Two years into the effort, someone stepped up and made it possible to lease that building for $1 a year. At the time I talked with its founder, Victory Health Partners was eighteen years into its mission, with more than 24,000 patients of record and a comprehensive total of $20 million worth of care provided.

So, who are those 24,000 patients, anyway? Lightfoot says most are between forty and sixty-five years old and suffering from chronic conditions like diabetes, heart disease or high blood pressure—chronic but treatable conditions that can be managed before they become life-threatening emergencies. Without the clinic, these folks wind up in a health crisis in either an urgent care or a hospital emergency room, where the damage from their health problems would be more severe and costlier to address. Instead, Victory Health even has a medication program that helps people tap into the low-income assistance drug firms are required to provide. Also, medical specialists have partnered with the clinic, enabling patients to visit physicians like cardiologists or orthopedists at a modest cost. With their health concerns under control, some of those patients are able to advance to better jobs—jobs with insurance.

"I'm the only doctor in Mobile who is glad to see their patients leave, and that's because they leave when they've got insurance," Lightfoot says.

Case Study

PIPES DON'T FAIL ME NOW

SHOW TITLE: *Carla Williams Wouldn't Let Her Dreams Die. Now She's Poised for a Huge Album Release.*

RELEASE DATE: *June 7, 2021*

Sometimes, never giving up requires an investment of years, lots of years. Just ask singer Carla Williams.

Carla first sang on a stage at her church when she was three years old, and she's never gotten it out of her blood. In a youth-dominated work culture, this forty-three-year-old mother of four decided she wouldn't give up on dreams of a music career. And how she has gone about that demonstrates that a never-give-up philosophy doesn't prohibit pausing for a decade or so.

"Everybody in the industry looks for those eighteen-year-olds who can be molded into what they want them to be," Carla says. But instead of a pliable teenager, she was a thirty-year-old mother of three when she cut her first album and started barnstorming from radio station to radio station in support of it.

"You have such a big dream and such a big goal that you think you can make it work. But I never would leave my children for more than two nights, ever. Back then that was a pivotal point. I would do what I could do out of Mobile," Carla says.

But it got to be too much, she acknowledges. "I needed a break; I needed to be Mom. I didn't want to miss one single minute of their lives," she says of her children. Also, she had a role in her family's contracting business. And so came the decision to put the music career aside for a while.

But she didn't give up. She *paused*. That's a crucial difference. And when she got to be about forty, she realized it was time to start that music career climb again.

"I've been able to figure out how to find the balance between having a family and being a successful artist, or at least trying to get back to being a successful artist," she says today.

Country music had always been her preferred genre, but as she rebooted her career, a strange thing happened. An industry veteran who had worked with the Carpenters—the '70s and '80s brother-and-sister duo—remarked that her voice had an uncanny resemblance to Karen Carpenter's. Carla was flattered by the compliment since Karen Carpenter's voice is so distinct and beloved. Then, it happened a second time—another industry veteran who had also worked with the Carpenters made the same remark. An idea was born.

As of this writing, *Carla Williams: A Tribute to the Carpenters* is poised for release. In keeping with changing tastes and technology for marketing and buying recordings, the fifteen Carpenters' cover songs will be released a few at a time over several months. Leading the pack and released in late 2021 was her favorite Carpenters' Christmas song, "Merry Christmas, Darling," done as a duet with veteran country singer Billy Dean.

"There's just so much about music that completes me on a daily basis," Carla says. "It's really what I've always known I was meant to do and what I knew deep down in my soul would one day work out."

I've heard her sing, and I wouldn't bet against her.

"To me, it is all about living with no regret," Carla told me when I interviewed her for *What's Working* in the Deep Fried studios.

And that comment drove it home for me. That's why you never give up. Otherwise, you will always live fearing regret. You will always wonder if you stopped too soon, maybe one step short of achieving your dream.

So there you have it, my case for never giving up. My evidence is four people reflecting on their businesses who have beaten the odds by not quitting. Each of them found ways to keep going. I've learned through my interviews that a winning formula includes a never-give-up attitude. When you hit an obstacle, you work through it—be it once or eighteen times.

WHAT WORKS

→ If starting a business was easy, many more would succeed. It's going to take some effort and persistence.

→ Every enterprise has fits and starts. Don't let the fits stop you in your tracks.

→ If a first attempt or approach doesn't work, there is probably another path, or two or three, to your goal.

→ If everyone doesn't love your idea immediately, that doesn't mean it's wrong. Find the right audience.

→ Confidence and passion for your products and services can help you find your way to "Yes."

5

BUILD A TEAM

The right team produces more than the sum of its members.

*I*f team building is essential to business success, you'd think American businesses would be pretty good at it, wouldn't you? But, by and large, we aren't. Part of it is scale working against us—the same specialization that enables a company to build a complex product, market it and distribute it naturally leads to silo-building. Factor in management that might not understand its role, ego, human nature, cultural and language barriers, poor communication skills, and you begin to see how people who might have the same goal still find it difficult to work together as a team.

The business world has made a business out of team-building advice. The speakers' circuit, the seminar world, specialty consultants, an entire library of business books—all of these tackle the topic. The fact that all of these approaches still exist proves that no one has actually solved the question of how to build a good team.

But what if we are going about it all wrong? What if the answer is not to be found in a particularly efficient factory, an especially highly regarded hospital, or a meteorically rising tech company? What if we are looking in the wrong places for best practices to copy when it comes to how to work together? What if the answer has been around since one of mankind's earliest artistic endeavors—on stage? In other words, what if Broadway could teach Wall Street a thing or two about working together?

That's a thought that came to me as I mined my treasure trove of interviews, looking for folks who understand team building. I embrace the mantra of "Find good people, empower them and get out of the way." Talking with a Tony Award-winning actor gave me some startling insights into how to take that mantra and make it an action plan.

I found plenty of other team-building expertise among those I've interviewed, as well. Especially outstanding examples included good friends-turned-business partners in the high-tech world of construction admixtures, and a hunting and fishing enthusiast who recognized an unserved market among those who share his passions.

Case Study

HE'S A REAL CHARACTER. REALLY.

SHOW TITLE: *Tony Award-Winning Actor Frank Wood on Quickly Creating High-Performing Teams*

RELEASE DATE: *August 2, 2021*

But since I started with my Broadway-teaching-Wall-Street analogy, let's talk about actor Frank Wood first.

I first thought about getting Frank on my show after I read an article from one of my regular rounds of business magazines, an article on "spontaneous teaming."

Spontaneous teaming works like this: A company pulls together a group of folks who have never worked together, people chosen for very unique or specific capabilities, and assigns them one specific, narrow task. Once that task is complete or that problem is solved, the team dissolves, as it was never intended to be a permanent thing anyway.

I love the concept. It sounds like something out of the military, a very mission-oriented approach. But it made me think of something else, too—performing in a play. Groups of people from a variety of fields and specialties—actors, directors, makeup artists, lighting technicians, and so on—come together to bring their different and specific skills to focus on a single mission: the production of a play. Now, that play may run a single night or the thirty-five-plus years that *Les Mis* has enjoyed in London. But blockbuster or flop, getting that play off the page and onto the stage took the work of a spontaneous team.

Spontaneous teams are also at work in movies. If you've ever stayed in your seat as the lights came up in a movie theater and watched the end credits roll, you have some idea of the army of people involved in the production of a movie. And yes, that's a spontaneous team. You don't really see the credits so much on a television show, and it's not the one-and-done of a movie, but it is still a spontaneous team.

To learn how the creative community so readily forms these spontaneous teams, I turned to my friend Frank. Now, Frank Wood's name may not be instantly recognizable, but his face just might be. He's been in so many television episodes and movies and stage productions, you are bound to have encountered him in at least some of them. And he's that rare hat trick of an actor, someone who works regularly in television, movies and on stage. I didn't ask him which venue he prefers, but from his comments, it's safe to say he favors the stage. And he's been around the world on it, too—including Broadway, London, Australia, and Ireland.

First, I asked him how he ended up in the acting business at all, since he has no tales of waiting tables while waiting on his big break.

"In my case, it took a supportive family," Frank says. "I came from a family with means and went debt-free through grad school."

That same family produced his sister, Maggie Hassan, who became first a lawyer, then governor of New Hampshire, then a U.S. senator.

After grad school, he performed in church basements and snooker halls on a theater tour through Ireland. He then put in a two-year stint at the People's Light and Theatre Company, a professional non-profit theater company in Pennsylvania via contacts with one of his former New York University professors. Then it was back to New York to establish himself as a working actor. In 1999, he won the Tony Award—Broadway's highest honor—as best featured actor for his role in *Side Man*, a Warren Leight play set in the jazz world.

And all the while, Frank has been working—not stop-gap jobs between acting gigs, but as a full-time working actor. By my internet-based count, he has appeared in at least twenty-nine movies between 2000 and now, including *Joker*, *The Royal Tenenbaums*, and *The Taking of Pelham 123*. My favorite among the things I've seen him in was his recurring role in seventeen of the twenty-two episodes of the late, great HBO series *Flight of the Conchords*. He also frequents episodic television, with guest roles including three different iterations of the *Law and Order* franchise, *Grey's Anatomy*, *The Sopranos*, *Modern Family*, *Bull*, *Mozart in the Jungle*, and *Evil*. With that variety from procedurals to sitcoms to supernatural (and that's just a sample), you're bound to have stumbled across him somewhere on your television.

So, Frank has been through this spontaneous teaming process hundreds of times. It starts, especially for plays, he says, with a group meeting around a table to read through a script and each actor or other participant working to mesh what they do with the director's leadership.

The process involves listening to fellow cast members (who would be called teammates in the business world) and then taking direction from the director (team leader in our environment), taking a strong position on your character (in business, your role on the team), and accepting redirection or refocusing when the director feels there is something better you can contribute.

"All of this is contingent on you being able to listen," Frank adds. "Sometimes you assert something, and the director says 'alright, no, let's just move forward.' You start listening because you don't know where you are and you start listening to what other people are saying, and when you go home that night, you are wondering 'Why did I think that?'"

When I asked for a particular experience where the team meshed best, it's not surprising he mentions *Side Man*, where he won his Tony. He says, "We had plenty of struggles, but we were a group of actors, all within about ten years of the same age. The director was strong and opinionated, and the playwright hadn't finished writing the play, he was writing it as we went along. We were just so in love with our own journey, the journey being the success of this play. We were new enough to it that we didn't have experience with this kind of success."

"Actors can famously disagree and be contentious, but that is really not the rule, that is more the exception," he says.

What I take away from that interview is that actors like Frank argue for the voices of their characters, but they're willing to move on when their director makes a ruling. That must be the way team members work in these spontaneous teams.

Case Study

THEN ADD A SPOONFUL OF FOREVER
TO THE MIX

SHOW TITLE: *M2 Solutions—Beth Morrissette and Andrea Moore—"You Build It, We Make It Last"*

RELEASE DATE: *July 5, 2020*

I got another lesson in team building by hearing how two long-term friends formed a business partnership and divided their responsibilities based on one another's strengths and experience.

Beth Morrissette and Andrea Moore are co-owners of M2 Solutions, a Mobile-based company that sells additives that make long-term construction materials—concrete, steel, paint—even more long-term, adding decades of utility to buildings and bridges.

The two friends wound up in business together one day when Beth had to cancel attending an event they'd planned to visit together so she could attend a program—on rust.

"Then I called her back and said, 'I have this interesting opportunity.' I was like, 'It's math and science! Come work with me—you love math and science!'" Beth says.

From that idea, M2 Solutions was born, to capitalize on the developing world of technologically advanced concrete admixtures that make construction projects more durable and last longer.

Beth was—and is—the CEO of Manufacturers Packaging Services, and the partners originally founded their business as a division of that company before taking it completely separate a few years later.

Now, before I go any further, I have to acknowledge that I was a bit surprised to see two women flourishing in the male-dominated world of construction. They didn't get huffy when I asked if their gender presented obstacles when the business launched, but they sounded sort of unfazed about it.

"It's really about trust. We've been around long enough that people know we know what we're doing," says Beth. The fact that the company launched within an established business with longevity and a good reputation helped early on, she adds.

"We don't get the strange looks we used to get when we first started out," Andrea says.

Beth is a business grad from the University of Alabama and was already CEO of Manufacturers Packaging Services when M2 Solutions was launched. Andrea is an engineering major from Vanderbilt who had several years of management experience with Black & Decker before becoming COO/ President of M2 Solutions.

"Because there are two of us, we have defined roles very clearly. When we go into technical discussions, I do the technology and Beth describes the business aspects," says Andrea.

But when you talk to the partners, it's clear that there's plenty of business savvy and technical know-how on both sides of the team.

"We love the people we work with, and helping them find solutions to complicated products has been really, really fun. It's been a great business model for us," Beth says.

Those solutions include better and faster ways to cure concrete, reducing costs while adding years to a project's lifespan, and even earning LEED (Leadership in Energy and Environmental Design) credits for biofriendly products and methods.

I didn't really press the partners for a list of projects on which they have worked, but among them are the Mississippi Aquarium and The Lodge at Gulf State Park Hotel and Convention Center.

The development of advanced admixtures that change the nature of building components is also changing the way construction works. Contractors, engineers and architects are finding themselves working together more as a team than previously, Andrea notes.

Whenever I talk to someone who has launched a new business successfully, I always like to ask them what they would do differently if they had a chance to go back and reboot. These two agreed they might have rethought putting their cell phone numbers out there quite so much.

"We had our ducks in a row, we had good legal support, we had good accounting support—but we never realized it would take us forever to get a city business license," says Beth.

Case Study

FISH ON! AND ON AND ON AND ON.

SHOW TITLE: *Huk and Nomad Brand Outdoor Performance Apparel—Josh Reed Spotted an Underserved Market*

RELEASE DATE: *March 15, 2021*

From the world of concrete and steel, we're going to move 180 degrees to talk about fishing spots and duck ponds and how a lifelong outdoorsman found a need and built a company to answer it.

Josh Reed is vice president of sales at Huk and co-founder of Marolina Outdoor, parent company to Huk and Nomad. Huk is high-performance apparel for the fishing enthusiast; Nomad is a wardrobe source for hunters.

You don't start from nothing and go to a brand name like Huk, which dominates the fishing world on social media, without an effective team. Josh had the advantage of starting out with a good team.

"I worked with a great crew in my past life and was introduced to a great crowd of people, basically a team, at Under

Armour. The relationships you build with people at work are like family—you have a family at home and a family at work," he says.

When Josh couldn't get Under Armour to embrace his idea that the fishing world was ready for high-end performance apparel, well, he was surrounded by a good team when he branched out on his own, and many of them came along for the ride.

Josh comes by his interest in the outdoors, particularly fishing, naturally.

"I grew up in South Carolina and at an early age I was exposed to what I call the swamp, catching catfish, catching garfish, which you don't want, from time to time. You name it. Those were aspects of growing up in the country and I understand the lifestyle," he says. "We're selling to a customer who is passionate about the outdoors. They're also conservationists. They hunt and fish and they want to be able to teach their children and their grandchildren to hunt and fish."

Now, when Josh tried to convince his former employers that there was an untapped market, they didn't get it, but some of his coworkers did. "They thought they (fishermen) want to spend money on beer and ice chests, not T-shirts. They have nice tackle, a nice rig, a nice bass boat and nice truck to pull it. Why not nice clothes?"

His former employer also hadn't caught on to the fact that fishing is a year-round activity. Boat sales may be seasonal in the spring and early summer, but fishing goes on twelve months out of the year. "With fishing, someone can get on a boat and they can go to a pond, they can go to a lake, they can go to a river, and fish where the best of the best fish. You have people who saltwater fish on the Gulf and around and up to Maine, and California's the same way," Josh says.

They were right about people being willing to invest in what they wore as well as what they fished with and from, but they did make one miscalculation.

"People are willing to spend money on the gear. But we thought we were going to sell a lot of graphic tees. By coming out with a performance line as well, it turned out the consumer wanted a long-sleeved performance shirt. They wanted good quality, something that was different and unique and that was not already in the marketplace," Josh says. "Our first shirt was a 90/10 poly-spandex body shirt that had a mesh background, basically a mesh back that was like an air conditioner. They were willing to spend 50 bucks, 55 bucks on a performance shirt, so we pivoted with planning."

As he considered taking a chance with his idea, Josh evaluated his own strengths and those of potential partners. He had experience selling to big-box stores—"the big accounts that can swing a big stick"—and a coworker had extensive contacts among independent retailers, who might possibly be more willing to take a risk on a new product.

"You have to figure out how you can take a product to market. Products come out every year and they flop because they don't have distribution," he says. By choosing a launch team with that in mind, he was on top of distribution from the outset.

Some of that original team from 2014 have moved on now, he notes. "You always remember where it started. The team we have now, I'm proud to be a part of them, but you always remember those you founded something with," he says.

So, I asked, has COVID changed your business?

"With COVID, more people are getting out of doors. They're looking for some protection against the elements. They see the Huk product we have developed and they think, 'That looks pretty cool, I'd like to own that.' It's very important that we stay on trend," Josh says.

When it came time to add hunting apparel to Marolina, Jason Hart—partner and now Josh's counterpart as vice president of sales at Nomad—chose the name because avid turkey hunters are nomads willing to travel anywhere to hunt turkeys, Josh says. The line has come up with camo that people can wear out and about every day, not just in the woods.

Assembling effective teams and then knowing enough to get out of their way and let them do their thing is both an art and a science. You see it in the way that a play comes together on a stage, that two friends set up a company that capitalizes on their separate strengths, and that entrepreneurs like Josh seek out like-minded individuals when they take the plunge into the marketplace.

Is spontaneous teaming a tool for your business? You have to admit it sounds intriguing, a potential way to capitalize on strengths—both known and unrecognized—among your employees. Just like you need long-term teams to run a business, maybe these task-oriented short-term versions serve a purpose.

—

WHAT WORKS

→ Working together as a team not only shares the load, it is a reward in itself.

→ No matter what you do, it's much easier to go to work when you feel like part of the team.

→ Team building is intentional. It doesn't just happen. You have work at it and sustain it.

→ Build a team with complementary skills and diversity of thought. Not a bunch of folks who all think and do alike.

→ Great teams are a productivity multiplier—they get way more done than just the sum of their members' efforts.

6

MASTER THE DETAILS

*Know your stuff
to set yourself apart.*

*C*ommand of detail impresses me. In a world where a depressingly large number of people think they know everything if you give them ninety seconds with Google, someone who really knows the precise details of their business is a breath of fresh air. Credibility is hard to come by today, but the CEO or the salesman or the front-desk jockey who knows the facts and figures that are the core of their work reeks of credibility. However, they're hard to find.

The people I interview are accomplished business owners or executives—their track record assures me that they know what they are doing. But I especially enjoy talking with people who have learned to control the buckets of information in their field. They convey confidence and expertise when they field questions without a single "I'll get back to you on that." After all, who would you rather buy a widget from, a salesman who says, "These are good widgets!" or one who can say "This widget performed 27 percent better in extreme weather conditions, as demonstrated by such-and-such study." (Of course, it goes without saying that if you checked up on that study, the information would hold up—details differ a lot from a smokescreen!)

When I started thinking about details and how they impact credibility, I considered some of the business leaders I'd spoken with who particularly stood out in their command of detail. I had plenty to choose from, since "detail-driven" is pretty much a given in a successful business executive. Maybe in the most sprawling corporation you will encounter a generalist who is propped up by the expertise of a large staff; but in the world of successful small businesses or other lean organizations, the folks in charge are detail folks.

I chose four people who struck me as especially good illustrations of the power of detail. They're from widely varied fields: a wholesale nursery exec, an entrepreneur who found an unmet need among dorm-frazzled parents, a financial advisor whose products include long-term care insurance, and an educator with a special perspective on educating boys. Each of them has a good handle on the trends in their particular fields—and the detailed backing for the projections they make (some of which are frightening). As I recount the stories each of these experts shared about their businesses, we'll see how details bolster their credibility.

Case Study

SUN + WATER + SOIL + WORK

SHOW TITLE: *Flowerwood Nursery—Growing and Delivering
Plants to Nurseries Across the Southeast*

RELEASE DATE: *September 20, 2021*

Let's start with Ellis Ollinger and Flowerwood Nursery, a family-owned firm that grew out of a retired lawyer named Harry Smith's hobby of breeding camellias and selling them. The sprawling wholesale nursery that has developed over the past eighty-plus years remains a family business. Ollinger is the CEO and while he is not himself family, he has worked there for thirty years and counting.

When we launched our interview, I was unprepared for how complex a commercial nursery business of this scale really is. Operating six sites spread out over three states calls for a grasp of plant patents, U.S. labor law as it applies to foreign workers, the impact of weather and climate, and gauging the shifting tastes of the American homeowner. And all of that's before you even begin discussing the science of making crops grow. It takes a moment to get your head around the fact that azaleas, camellias and holly are crops, just like cotton and soybeans.

And timing is of the essence in this business.

"If it rains, or there is a weather event like a late frost or a hurricane, we never get that customer back because the next weekend they are going to a football game or graduation or a spring-break trip. When we lose a weekend in the spring, we really see it in our sales," Ellis says. "We have a saying in this business: There's no problem that six perfect weather weekends in Atlanta won't solve."

Flowerwood offers its customers—primarily the big-box home improvement and garden stores you visit on your weekend rounds—810 different varieties of plants, some in three different sizes, Ellis says. But a core of about 250 of those varieties accounts for about 80 percent of the company's business.

"We try to put in front of the consumer the plant that we feel they are going to have the most success within their yard," he says.

In my career, I've done loads of research on the different consumer preferences and workplace habits of the different generations, and I was delighted to learn Ellis tracks that, too. The Baby Boomers are his biggest customer, but Millennials are coming on strong, and the pandemic seems to be pushing them outside the home office and into their gardens, he notes.

The type of plant that is in demand is evolving as America's suburbs evolve. Flowerwood cut its teeth on the sprawling lawns surrounding the ranch houses of the Baby Boomer, but that generation's now-grown offspring are living in bigger, often two-story houses on smaller lots. They have developed a taste for gardening, but their needs have changed.

"The new gardener wants a smaller plant, a more compact plant. They want blooms—if there's no blooms, there's no room in their garden. They want a functional plant. They are big on edibles like blueberries and tomatoes, and we don't really do edibles. To fit what we do well, our plant and our plant-development sister company have concentrated on new plants that solve a problem in the landscape, including a lot of dwarf varieties of things like loropetalum (fringe flower). They love that it is a different color than green, and it stays small, more of a garden look than a ton of shrubs," Ellis says.

"So," I ask, "If there's a need in the landscape, what do you do—go into a lab and create a plant?" And that's where Ellis offers me a lesson on the complex world of patenting a living plant.

"Most of the plants that we develop come from hobby gardeners or breeding houses that do a little higher level. They bring them to us and say, 'This bush has been growing well in my yard for years.' We trial it for years to make sure it stays stable and that we like the attributes, and that it can be grown in a commercial environment," he says.

Perhaps there's no better—or more profitable—example than the Encore Azalea, a patented azalea that blooms in spring, summer and fall, unlike traditional azaleas which are glorious for a week and done for the year. Ellis tells the tale of a hobby breeder in Independence, Louisiana, who was crossbreeding azaleas and rhododendrons and came up with a multi-season bloomer. The breeder, Robert "Buddy" Lee, approached Flowerwood with his find and the two agreed to split the patent fee. Encore entered the market in the late 1990s, to great success. "Now we sell almost four million plants a year. Buddy continues to breed new varieties of

Encore and other plants for us. He's a wonderful spokesman for the breeds he has developed," Ellis says.

"Branding is something that allows the grower to create product for the consumer," Ellis says.

Nothing succeeds like success, and the smashing launch of the Encore brand drew the right kind of attention for Flowerwood. The late John Floyd, who had become editor-in-chief of the iconic *Southern Living* magazine in the early 1990s, approached the company, looking for a growing partner to create a plant brand bearing the magazine's name. A most successful partnership was formed.

"For the *Southern Living* line, the plants must be unique, solve a problem in the landscape; they're typically unique to our brand and are just a superior plant," Ellis says.

To document the resiliency of American business, you need look no further than those businesses and industries that thrived during the pandemic years of 2020 and 2021. And growth, however welcome, can create its own problems.

"The pandemic has created strong demand for our products. As people stayed home, they looked around and began to garden. It caught our supply chain by surprise," Ellis says. The demand accelerated so much, he added, that the limited number of manufacturers for nursery containers—domestic companies based in Florida, Ohio, the Carolinas, California, and Texas—were caught unprepared, and it became a challenge to find the pots to put their plants in. Even the pot business has become more complicated: Instead of the nondescript and unimportant colors of the previous generation of nursery containers, the increasing number of branded plants come with their own requirements—purple ones for Encore, earth-tone brown for the *Southern Living* line.

Flowerwood Nursery has four locations in Alabama, another in Georgia, and one in Florida, where the growing season gives them a four- to six-week head start over Alabama's Gulf Coast. All those facilities create a large demand for labor, and much of it is seasonal.

"To say we are seasonal would be an understatement. We do 65 to 75 percent of our business between February 15 and Mother's Day. We have to bulk up 20-plus percent of our labor, and we try to carry as much of our expertise labor as long as we can," Ellis says, with the spring workforce booming to 650 or more. The demand for labor outstrips the supply, and the company cannot always hire all the domestic help it needs, he adds.

"With the H-2A Program (Temporary Agricultural Employment of Foreign Workers), you can hire guest workers if you can show you have a need that cannot be met domestically. We depend on that. Company-wide, we use about 150 guest workers," he says, primarily coming from Mexico and Central America.

Legally employing these workers is a complex task that calls for months of advertising for U.S. workers, placing a work order with the Department of Labor, and making arrangements for housing and health care, he says.

Who knew that ornamental horticulture on a major commercial scale could be so complex? Well, we know now.

Do you see how Ellis' use of detail drives home his points and establishes him as an authority? Details carry power.

Case Study

AN EDUCATION BEFORE
THE SCHOOLING STARTS

SHOW TITLE: *Not Just Dorms: An Entrepreneurial Business That Makes Dorm Decoration Quick, Pretty, and Lightweight*

RELEASE DATE: *September 9, 2019*

Or consider the case of Shawn Cushing. She was running other family businesses when she stumbled across an opportunity during the backbreaking labor of moving her oldest daughter into a dorm room at the University of Alabama. That's where Not Just Dorms got its start, offering an upscale and lightweight take on dorm furnishings and decor.

Moving a college freshman out of the nest and into the dorm is a challenge, Shawn acknowledges. "It's tiring. You pack up, load up, unpack, organize and then leave! Move-in is emotional and strenuous. This is not the time to try to put an IKEA item together," she says.

Have you seen a college dorm room lately? They are not the Spartan things that Baby Boomers remember from years past. Some families even go so far as to bring in a decorator. Not Just Dorms provides a middle ground—customized furnishings and soft goods to give a dorm a luxe and comfortable look.

Shawn's criteria? Her products must be lightweight, durable and damage-free, because parents don't want to pay for damage to walls from overzealous attachments. The weight requirement is the most stringent, because these goods are primarily hauled by the parents alone.

"I tried everything. I tried plywood. I tried corkboard. I tried pegboard. I tried foam alone. I tried plastic. It had to be lightweight but it also had to not bend—plywood's going to warp. I ultimately found THE product—a laminate base board used in flooring construction," Shawn says.

The basis of a decorated dorm room requires two products, she says: a headboard constructed of the above-mentioned laminate and covered with padded fabric, and a bedskirt mounted with tension rods to hide the storage under elevated dorm beds. From there, families can go further, with matching fabric poufs, throw pillows and other décor elements. There's even a lightweight recliner she hopes catches on, although she says it hasn't so far.

Not Just Dorms would typically outfit five hundred to six hundred dorm rooms each fall, 75 percent of them at large Southern universities, she says. She sold the company in 2021, after our interview.

Case Study

GET THE FINAL DETAILS RIGHT

SHOW TITLE: *Long-Term Care—How It Works and Why You Need to Know About It*

RELEASE DATE: *August 9, 2021*

As one generation is moving into their first home-away-from-home in a dormitory, another is contemplating its future in a world where we may well outlive our health and our savings. Jay Stubbs of Concourse Financial Group in Mobile, Alabama, is the detail-oriented expert who explained to me and my listeners the options and shortcomings of long-term care products. Here's where his command of detail really impressed me, as well as terrified me.

Jay describes himself as passionate about the ways the products he handles protect assets and lifestyles, be it life insurance, disability insurance or long-term care insurance. It is the last of these that was the focus of our discussion on *What's Working*.

"I ask people a series of questions. Do you have a plan in place to protect your assets and your family dynamic if you cannot take care of yourself? And if you don't have a plan, does that concern you?" Jay says.

It should. Lifespans are getting longer. The insurance business is the most data-driven, detail-oriented business there is, and Jay says you can now buy a life insurance policy that will cover you to the age of 125.

Jay can speak to each of the details needed to create a plan for his clients, as each of them has subtleties that the client needs to understand. The details on the client range from age, to marital status, to current age or death age of parents, to tobacco user, to medications they take. Then there are the details needed to customize a plan like budget, where the money is coming from to fund the plan, to how long they anticipate needing any benefit, to inflation considerations, and on and on. Each one of these details has significance to the plan and Jay knows them all.

"Typically, we were having this conversation with people at retirement, and now we're having conversations with people in their mid-forties and early fifties," Jay said.

As he went on to explain, there are four ways to protect yourself from long-term care expenses: self-insurance, in which you set aside money in your accounts or portfolio to cover that eventuality; traditional long-term care coverage, which is usually exhausted two to six years after you claim it; asset-based long-term care coverage, which involves leveraging a smaller amount of investment; and traditional life insurance with a rider that allows you to draw against the death benefit for use in a care facility or at home.

And to drive home the bottom line here, Jay points out the availability to the public of the Genworth Cost of Care study (genworth.com). This free website gives you an accurate picture of the cost in your specific community for various levels of care: in-home, assisted living and nursing home, and even allows you to see the projections for the next thirty years.

"The budding reality is that many of us will be caring for people in our family in ways we did not anticipate," Jay says.

Case Study

MAN-CHILD

SHOW TITLE: *The Hidden, Undiscussed Crisis of Boys: Educator Blair Fisher Discusses a Growing Concern*

RELEASE DATE: *July 12, 2021*

I do a lot of work with the financial advising community, and when they ask me what the future holds, I say it is going to be female dominated in affluence-building because the behaviors of affluence-building are largely being captured and demonstrated by females more than males. I learned there's more meat to this prediction when I interviewed Blair Fisher, head of school for St. Paul's Episcopal School in Mobile, who can describe how today's schools are now consistently failing male students and setting society up for some very unpleasant consequences.

Blair offered these details: In 1970, males accounted for 58 percent of college enrollment. In 2020, 60 percent of the enrollment was female. In graduate education, by the year 2030, experts predict two-thirds of the enrollment will be female. Where are the guys going? The answer, for too many of them, is nowhere.

"When a young boy begins school, he enters a highly feminized environment—one dominated overwhelmingly by female teachers. Statistically speaking, he is likely to have only female teachers throughout elementary school, and usually early middle school as well. He will start to see some male teaching influence in late middle school and more so in high school," Blair says. "While I am speaking in generalities, of course, men and women process reality differently: Thus, male and female teachers organize their classes and their education approach based on what 'feels right' to them. Therefore, it's only natural that a feminized learning environment tends to be more conducive to female success. For multiple physiological and developmental reasons, boys tend to be more active, competitive, louder, and are unable to sit still for long periods of time. Girls mature earlier than boys do. That's just a fact. They are able to maintain attention typically longer than boys. They also tend to want to please the authority figures in their life. In a typical classroom, the environment rewards girl-typical behavior and punishes boy-typical behavior. The result is that for many boys, education begins to feel like a game they can't win. The statistics completely bear this out," Blair says.

Now, I hear the Baby Boomers in my audience thinking that this doesn't sound so different from the classrooms they grew up in. But there's a key difference today, and Blair points it out: With the rapid growth of single-parent homes (overwhelmingly single mothers), there are far fewer positive male role models in children's lives.

Blair relates what research makes clear: "The single biggest factor that influences how well boys do in school is the presence of a strong positive male role model. This modeling of positive masculinity is important for girls to develop in a healthy manner as well, but for boys it is absolutely crucial."

He recommends that single mothers ensure that their sons and daughters are exposed regularly to such modeling and that our education system intentionally encourages and rewards men who enter the teaching profession. Other measures he advocates are the importance of preserving recess and giving children an opportunity to move during the school day, as well as experimenting with single-gender classes, explicitly training teachers on how to organize their classrooms and approaches in ways that meet the needs of both girls and boys, and holding them accountable for both female and male success.

If this crisis is not addressed, the future looks lonely, he says.

"Women tend to want to partner equal or up in the social hierarchy. It's a normal phenomenon that is consistently demonstrated across time and cultures. We have a growing pool of successful women, which is a terrific thing, because we have intentionally sought to "program" for their success in recent decades. But projecting forward, they are going to have a smaller and smaller pool of successful men to partner with because much of the societal reprogramming has been through a zero-sum approach," he says.

Blair cites data sets that show the extent of the crisis: Boys drop out at a rate more than twice that of girls; boys account for 70 percent of the Ds and Fs which teachers award and are twice as likely to be suspended; girls dominate enrollment in Advanced Placement courses, student government, and academic awards. Projecting forward, the prison population—overwhelmingly male—is also overwhelmingly full of fatherless men who failed at school.

Can you see the extent to which Blair's use of detail clarifies that there really is a crisis in the education of boys today, and the dangers that crisis poses to all of us?

These four executives come from widely different corners of the business world, but their use of detailed information in making their points is a shared attribute. Claim that attribute for yourself, as well, and master the details that drive your own business. Sure, we all delegate work to our subordinates and associates. But we cannot delegate to anyone the absolute necessity of owning the details of our work.

→

WHAT WORKS

→ "Know your stuff" is a much better bet than "Fake it 'til you make it."

→ Expertise and mastery of detail set you apart as a business or an employee—it's worth the effort.

→ The devil *is* in the details, and if you don't master them, he just might get ya.

+ A web search does not confer expertise. Learn the difference between real research and clickbait.

+ Deep understanding of the details of your business gives you a competitive advantage and an accurate picture of where you stand.

7

BE RESILIENT

*Overcome challenges and grow stronger
with lessons learned.*

Business is hard. Even in flush economic times, business is hard. Even when your business is making money and growing, business is hard. Even when your family life is in perfect sync with your work life, business is hard. And since the economy isn't always good and your business isn't always prospering and your family life isn't always perfect, business can be doubly hard.

And when something is hard, the idea of quitting sneaks in. Days confront you when quitting seems like the best idea. Business partners may disappoint you, a competitor's ethical lapses may be flagrant, the sheer number of hours your work demands may be exhausting. I discuss in another chapter the "never-give-up" mentality that drives successful businesses, but here I'm discussing the coping strategies when things get hard—which they will. Staying on top of your emotions will get you through the hard part. The question is, how do you do that?

When I was combing through my interviews, thinking which guests had best addressed how to stay strong in difficult times, I was struck by one thing: The two people who most clearly articulated ways to stick it out through adversity are also arguably the best-known experts I've interviewed, and I think that speaks to the urgency and universal need for their message.

Now, small-business owners are the backbone of the American economy. Whether their product is high-end boutique bacon or a patented species of azalea, they create jobs within their community and feed the enormous American consumer appetite. But outside their companies and their small towns, they are not known quantities. They walk through airports without being recognized. There's probably not a household name among them. But when it comes to Amy Morin and Thom Shea, well, the circle of people who recognize those names is much broader.

Amy is a psychotherapist and Thom is a retired Navy SEAL. Both have several books to their credit, and both are genuine rock stars on the speakers' circuit, where I live a big part of my professional life.

Case Study

A HEAD LIKE A ROCK

SHOW TITLE: *Thirteen Things Mentally Strong People Don't Do*
RELEASE DATE: *March 22, 2021*

At the time I interviewed Amy, her TEDx Talk on mental strength had fifteen million views; last I checked, it was up to nineteen million. The eyeballs keep hitting that video clip because she has some experience-based and practical advice about what NOT to do in order to develop mental strength.

"Most people don't know what mental strength is. It's not about adding more stuff to your to-do list, but it can be about taking a few things off," Amy says. "Mentally strong people don't focus on things they can't control. This is really about identifying what is within our control and what isn't. We can control how we think, how we feel and how we behave, but we cannot control other people."

To that list of things beyond personal control, add things like government regulations and—a timely example—the pandemic.

"You can't control people. You can help motivate them, but know that at the end of the day, if they fall short it is not your fault. You cannot force someone to behave in a certain way," Amy says. "It's smart to have a plan, but it's just not wise to put all your effort into thinking you're going to prevent the storm from coming. The more you let go of control, the more you get. It's one of the great paradoxes: Our desire to control limits what we can control."

Amy comes to her insights via a road of hard experience, even though her professional life started out smooth and pretty. At twenty-three, fresh out of graduate school as a licensed clinical social worker, she thought she had it all: newly married, newly employed as a psychotherapist, owner of a new home. Then her mother, with whom she had been particularly close, died unexpectedly of an aneurysm. Three years later, her twenty-six-year-old husband died without warning of a heart attack. Early in life and in a profession dedicated to helping others cope, Amy found herself struggling to come to terms with the fact that life isn't fair.

She found some answers in her practice. Some of those who came to her for help were bitter and angry, and others were hopeful, she noticed. "What separated these people was more about what they didn't do than what they did," she says. "I learned a lot of unhealthy habits to avoid. If you give up one bad habit, all these good habits you have will be that much more effective."

She wrote a blog about that insight and posted it. "Fifty million people read it and it changed the course of my life," is how she puts it. And just like that, Amy became America's mental strength coach, another overnight success after years of painful work.

That blog became her bestselling book, *13 Things Mentally Strong People Don't Do*. And Amy is generous with her observations. You don't even have to buy the book to read the list; she spells them out on her website, amymorinlcsw.com. That sample may well spur you to go for the longer read, and for her subsequent books, *13 Things Mentally Strong Parents Don't Do* and *13 Things Mentally Strong Kids Do* (a reversal on her usual naming practice, she says, because a young person pointed out to her that kids are generally done with being told what not to do), and others.

Amy advises to recognize your bad habits, decide what to replace them with, and then implement that decision.

"It has to do with the way you think, the way you feel, and the way you behave. So, for instance, if you are someone that always beats yourself up, maybe you call yourself names or you speak really harshly to yourself, you have to recognize that you are doing that and then decide how you are going to behave differently," she says. It can be as simple as giving up sitting on the couch thinking about how bad things are and instead getting up and calling a friend.

Jealousy is another bad habit that saps mental strength, she says. For examples here, she turns to businesses in different states during the pandemic. Some businesses were allowed to remain open in some states, but those in other states were not. Some businesses got favorable government-backed loans; others didn't. Some businesses saw their competitors breaking pandemic rules and making money from it.

"A lot of this was a roll of the dice. We couldn't have predicted the pandemic," she says. So instead of resorting to jealousy and wasting "limited mental real estate" on that negative feeling, she says, acknowledge the situation as beyond your control.

When people start to think about habits, they get anxious. Most of us, myself included, have struggled with breaking habits and we know it is hard work and frequently fails. After all, if everyone could quit smoking on the first try, quitting smoking would not have become an entire industry. And speaking of habit-breaking becoming an industry, look at the wealth of weight-loss solutions that solve nothing! So, people have good reason to worry when told they need to break bad habits. But the time involved need not be staggering, Amy says.

"Some people spend forty years getting into a bad habit. We're not going to change that entire habit in two weeks, but we can start chipping away at it in two weeks," she says. "For those who double down, change is quick. Others, working in small periods of time, it takes longer. Some need more guidance or more coaching because they are dealing with a difficult home situation or a non-supportive work environment."

In other words, breaking a habit varies with the individual, but added effort brings quicker results.

While I had the chance, I couldn't resist asking Amy if her practice brings her a single, recurring problem from those who come to her for help. And, yes, it does: "People who don't want to confront someone in their own life—a business partner who disappoints them or a mother-in-law who is mean to them—they'll ask, 'Can I bring this person into your office and you tell them, or can you write them a letter?'" she says. From just the little you've learned about

Amy here, I guess you can tell she declines to do those people's work for them, although she'll help them develop the skills to do it themselves.

Case Study

THE ENERGIZER BUNNY AIN'T
GOT NOTHIN' . . .

SHOW TITLE: *Thom Shea—Retired Navy SEAL—Now Coaches Execs to be the Best Version of Themselves*

RELEASE DATE: *February 15, 2021*

Now, mental strength is not as obvious as physical strength. Amy and I talked about how you can see a person's biceps and know they are physically strong, but there are often no exterior signs that someone is mentally strong. But there is a case where you can take it for granted that someone is strong in both ways: if they are a Navy SEAL.

The prowess of the Navy SEALs, even more so than the other U.S. special forces, is the stuff of folklore and fodder for screens both large and small. I saw the respect the general public has for these special warriors when I saw how Thom Shea could fill a meeting hall on the speakers' circuit. What really impressed me was how everyone—myself included—hung on his words. How does he do it?

Now retired after twenty-three years as a SEAL, Thom writes books and shares his leadership secrets in books, speeches and the Unbreakable Leadership seminars he and his wife teach. It's a second career he had not envisioned, expecting instead to follow a more conventional post-military path as, perhaps, a security consultant.

"I was going to either die in the teams or go so long they had to pull me out," Thom told me. He worked fifty-eight combat missions and ran out of food, water and ammunition on each, so he made a practice of writing letters home to his kids, offering them guidance against the time he might not be there. But a 2009 mission he led in Afghanistan left him feeling he'd had his "Super Bowl" moment and he was free to consider civilian life. And that civilian life began with a book, *Unbreakable: A Navy SEAL's Way of Life*.

The way Thom tells it, he had no interest in writing a book, but his wife Stacy had other plans. She had saved those letters her husband had sent the family from the battlefield, and they became the basis of that first book.

Getting into the SEALs is a battle in itself: The rigor of their training and selection process is legendary. And Thom says he didn't exactly graduate at the head of his first class.

"I have a disease called 'I don't give up,'" says Thom. "I am the only one who has been allowed to try it five times. Usually, they only let you try it twice."

"How you feel regarding capability is probably not the greatest metric. I never felt I wasn't going to make it. I stopped interacting with what my brain thought was possible. I just started interacting with the nuances of the next five inches, how can I move to the corner, how can I move the next two minutes. You have to move; you have to not give up."

Many years later, when he himself was an instructor for the introductory course, from 2001 to 2004, he remembers being advised not to try to predict who would make it and who wouldn't. "You just deliver the program to them and let them evaluate themselves," he says.

As of this writing, the introductory version of Thom's Unbreakable Leadership training starts at $6,000. That may well have changed by the time you read this, but you get the point—it ain't cheap. Yet in his remarks on the speakers' circuit and in his interview with me, Thom freely gives away the foundation of his course.

Thom says, "I found you have to create a foundation, and that foundation is learning these two concepts. It takes about eight hours to learn them, and then a month to apply them. It is learning viscerally. Honoring your word is the foundation of human life. You are what comes out of your mouth and what you think about. Until you learn that, it is very hard to apply anything of value. And the second foundation is: Don't give up on that."

He illustrates the process with a hypothetical twenty-one-day assignment. Imagine you were told to do ten sit-ups, ten push-ups and ten squats immediately on waking up and right before getting in bed, for twenty-one days straight. It isn't an arduous workout—in fact, it doesn't really count as a workout at all. But virtually no one, he says, is successful. They forget, they want to rearrange the time, they don't feel well one day, and so on. "What we give credence to is honoring every reason not to," is how Thom puts it.

"Until you prove to yourself you can make a promise for twenty-one days and keep it, I can't teach you anything," he says. "The obstacle is the individual. If you can't beat the internal battle, you've already talked yourself out of it."

The ease of modern middle-class life may be hindering people from reaching their full potential, Thom believes. "Humans are capable of greatness. We don't ever stretch ourselves in the world because things are comfortable. We don't stretch ourselves unless we live in central Africa, where things are not comfortable," he says.

My interview with Thom covered lots of ground, but my favorite take-away, the one that resonated the most with me, was this: "Drama prevents humans from being the best version of themselves."

In his world, drama sounds like another word for an excuse. "Everyone would have a different definition of that: Oh, you won't believe how bad it was, this didn't work out, this happened. Drama causes people to not be awesome."

Thom's courses and much of his speaker's work focus on the middle careers of those who have been successful in their earlier career phases, a dynamic that comes into play somewhere between ages thirty-five and fifty for most people. The question becomes whether to move on or stay stuck.

Moving from a SEAL's life to a civilian one was a major transition, and Thom points out it wasn't a quick process. "Transition is nothing that can be done overnight. It is not possible to do great things overnight," he says.

Thom's first book came out in 2015, and he's added a second since then, plus his podcast and additional writing. The Unbreakable Leadership course he and his wife teach had graduated 415 people at the time we last spoke. No, not an overnight transition, but a pretty awesome one.

Developing mental strength is an interesting process. Would Amy have discovered the strength-building practices she now shares with others had she not been hit with so many personal tragedies so early in her life? Would Thom have become the dynamic leader he eventually became if he had passed his first try at SEAL training, or if he had given up after his fourth attempt?

Those are unanswerable questions, but the answerable question is "Can we learn from their techniques?" and the answer is "Yes." We can replace destructive thought habits with positive ones. We can realize the importance of our words and our thoughts and put into practice the habit of never giving up. Just like I can lace up my running shoes and start working on my physical strength today, so can I start working on my mental strength.

Because I know I'll need it. Because, for all its rewards and fulfillment, as I said at the beginning of this chapter, business is hard.

WHAT WORKS

→ Adversity will happen. Be prepared, but also be willing to change course.

→ We are often the source of our own adversity. Work to overcome your inner obstacles.

→ Obstacles can be an excuse to fail or a challenge to overcome. Choice is yours.

→ Business, like life, is not easy or fair. Accept that and keep working toward your goals.

→ Overcoming challenges makes achievement more rewarding and fulfilling.

8

SERVE PEOPLE, NOT PRODUCT

Who you serve comes before
what you serve.

*I*n the *Wolf of Wall Street*, the title character (based on real-life stockbroker Jordan Belfort) offers a simple test for would-be salesmen. He hands them a pen and says, "Sell me this pen." Most begin touting the features of the pen. Fail. Problem is—maybe we don't need a pen. Or don't want one. The successful pen sales are based on a need or want for the pen in the customer. The point is, unless we take the time and care to understand our customers and clients, their wants and needs, we will not be able to deliver for them. Everyone who enters the marketplace has a want or a need or a problem to solve. Understand that problem and solve it, and you don't just have a sale, you have a long-term client. In my interviews with folks who are successful in sales and service, I found a common thread: They aren't just serving up product, they are serving people.

Case Study

CONNECT TO THE CLIENT

SHOW TITLE: *A Passion for People and Service: Cars Are Just the Product*

RELEASE DATE: *January 21, 2019*

Ty Bullard owns multiple car dealerships in and around L.A.—"lower Alabama." His dealerships span everything from luxury brands to Ford pickup trucks. About a thousand cars make up his inventory on any given day, and some of them he couldn't even drive off the lot because, although Ty has been knee-deep in automobiles for most of his life, he can't drive a stick shift.

It may sound strange that, since Joe Bullard Automotive's founding in 1955 by Ty's grandfather, they've never really been in the car business. They sell cars alright, and lots of them. Drive anywhere in and around Mobile and you'll see the family name in traffic, on Acuras, Jaguars, Land Rovers, you name it. But the business has thrived over three generations because each generation has understood they are really in the *service* business, not the car business. Their mission, though maybe not printed on the showroom wall, is to serve people. Cars are simply the vehicle (pun firmly intended) through which they do it. And of the most successful businesses I've had on the show, this is a common theme. And they don't just say it, they do it too. It's deep in the DNA of their culture. They hire and promote people based on their natural inclination to serve. And these companies also have the most loyal employees, the highest employee engagement, and the most loyal customers. There's something to it. And smaller companies seem to be able to live this way more than large ones; such is the case with Joe Bullard Automotive and, as we'll see shortly, United Bank. Ty's attitude toward finding new employees: Prove to me you know how to serve people. If you can, I'll teach you all you need to know about selling, fixing, and managing cars. (Oh, and by the way, spare a moment to appreciate the difficulties of the multi-generational family business—talk about pressure not to screw it all up!)

Maybe the car business is too easy an example for my argument that all businesses today are essentially service businesses. After all, an automobile is a purchase that requires ongoing service. But even when the service connection is more subtle—as in, say, the financial industry or real estate—the customer, the client, the prospect is coming to you to ask "Can you solve my problem? Can you fill my need?" That means the path forward is clear, even if you cannot drive a stick shift: A service ethic creates success.

Our businesses are merely the shell within which we serve people. That's become clear over my first two hundred radio guests. Repetition of this same message has created validation of that belief. But people struggle to say it outright: It's a simple yet radical concept that even my most well-spoken guests have difficulty articulating. Then came Ty with his "We are not car people" ethos and he laid it out exactly on those lines. And there was Bob Jones from the financial industry, echoing the same sentiments from the vantage point of a community bank. (Sit tight, more on him later.)

Here's a story Ty shared with me on the show that sums it up. He got a call from a guy who had gone fishing with his son and returned that evening too late and too tired to unload his SUV. The next morning, he went out to handle that chore and discovered that the drain plug on his cooler had been loose, and as the ice in the cooler melted overnight, his car interior became drenched in a fishy effluvium. He needed that car that day, and as the day wore on, the smell went from a stink to a stench. He was desperately searching for someone who could help de-stink his SUV, and everyone he'd called had declined to even try.

Is it possible to get the smell of fish meltwater out of a car's upholstery? Ty didn't know. But he told the car owner to bring the car in and his service team would give it a go. If the team was successful, Ty and the car's owner would agree on a price. If the smell had staying power, well, no charge, Ty told him. Now, I let Ty out of the interview that day without asking him how that story came out. But I know a more important outcome of that story: When it comes time for Fish Guy to buy his son his first car, where's he going to go?

That would be a nice, instructive business story at any time, but it is a particularly important story for today. Why? Because the auto industry has so many disruptors. No industry—literally, not a one—is immune from disruptors surfing in on new technology, but the auto sales industry had those disruptors sooner and in greater numbers than other places. Millennials, who are now in their twenties up to their forties, find nothing strange about buying a car online, much as they might buy a box of batteries or a new backpack for their kids. And those Millennials are going to influence their parents, their in-laws and their children. So, when Fish Guy's kid (who, by the way, got the blame for the leaky fish cooler) wants wheels of his own, there's already a relationship—however slight—that's way ahead of pixels and touch screens.

Put it this way: If your customer/client/prospect/man-on-the-street has a problem, you have an opportunity. The holder of that problem may think you are selling cars or groceries or dog-sitting, but what you (and every other business out there) are doing is serving people—specifically, in the form of problem solving. Remember, busyness (not business) is today's status symbol. Everyone is either time-pressed and time-stressed, or they think they are (which amounts to the same thing). Take a problem off their hands, and you gain a happy customer/client/convert.

"I think a lot of people probably dread a car-buying experience," Ty says, being brutally honest about it. "It's like 'Oh, I know I've gotta do it, I've gotta have a car, but gosh, I just don't want to go through this again.' So we've got a big focus now on what we call the customer journey."

That journey includes all customer touchpoints, not just the moment of the sale. It includes choosing a car, handling the financing and paperwork, bringing the car in for service, reminding the customer about scheduled maintenance and end-of-lease time lines, and—most importantly—resolving any problems that come up, be it a scratched fender or a fuel pump recall.

"A customer doesn't necessarily realize it's a journey, but we need to be aware that it is. People don't buy a car—they buy an experience. That's where the value is. It's when you have an issue and we're there taking care of it, that's where value is created—and that's important as we go forward into the digital world," says Ty.

With that in mind, his company has created "JB Driven," a leadership training program that focuses on teaching the customer journey and buffing up, among other things, communication skills among the staff. The goal, he says, is to put the brakes on the notorious churn among automotive dealership employees (especially sales staff) and make sure customers will see the same faces year after year. Those familiar faces add comfort to the customer journey.

Customers aren't the only ones fulfilled by a service approach. We all want something more than a paycheck for our efforts in the workplace. We want impact. And significance. Imagine yourself as the lead character in the Christmas classic, *It's a Wonderful Life*. When you get that magical opportunity to see what the world would be like without you, wouldn't you like to see some difference between the World With You and the World Without You? Those who approach their work as a life of serving people are the folks who make an impact in the world, one de-fishified SUV at a time.

Case Study
BANKING ON DOING
THE RIGHT THING

SHOW TITLE: *United Bank CEO Bob Jones—A Mission to Serve*
RELEASE DATE: *April 19, 2021*

Now, let's return to Bob Jones and United Bank. Bob may have the most generic, white-bread name in the phone book (there are some reading this who don't know what those are), but no one in or around Atmore, Alabama, wonders who he is. At the time of our interview, he was president and CEO of United Bank, based in Atmore, and he rose to that position after only two years with the bank and held that post from 1992 until retiring in the summer of 2021. Although publicly traded, United Bank is a community bank. Since we were just reminiscing about *It's a Wonderful Life*, that gives me an opportunity to point out Bob is much more like that movie's heroic George Bailey than Mr. Potter, the foreclosure-happy villain.

"There are a lot of banks in America, but nowhere else in major economies did community banks exist," Bob says. "That is the beauty of the community banking model. What happens is, when a business is in a strong position, they can get a loan anywhere. When they really need you, that option's not there."

Except, perhaps, with United Bank. And Bob can point to concrete examples, like the bank's experience with the federal Paycheck Protection Program, one of the emergency financial measures designed to help small businesses and their employees weather the potential financial ruin brought about by COVID-19. The U.S. Small Business Administration's PPP program helped businesses keep their workforce on the job during the pandemic—but the SBA program required participation from financial institutions for its loans. United Bank was among those that stepped up to take part.

During the program (which lapsed May 31, 2021), United Bank participated in 950 PPP loans, averaging $50,000. Averages don't really tell the story, though—the amounts varied from a low of $400 to a high of $2 million. But here's how Bob tells the heart of the story:

"Over 350 of those loans were to businesses that were not our customers previously. They could not get an institution to respond to them or help them with the process, or their institution chose not to participate. We stepped into the void and said 'No, this is important. These businesses will not make it through the COVID experience without this'—and so we offered it."

"That's what sets the community bank model apart. You can take the financials and you can analyze them, but [larger banks] cannot understand the spirit and the tenacity and the commitment of the principals [aka business owners], and the drive behind their commitment to weather difficult times," he says.

As a reader of a business book, I'm willing to bet you have at least a toehold in the American middle class. From that perspective, it's often hard to realize how hard financial life can be for the financially underserved. The U.S. already struggles with a financial literacy problem, so those least likely to recognize a predatory lender often have little other recourse but potential traps like payday loans with interest rates in excess of 400 percent. (I kid you not, more than 400 percent.) I bet you didn't even realize a person has to qualify for a checking account—and lots of people can't. Showing up with fifty dollars and a photo ID is no guarantee you're going to walk out of a bank as an account holder.

The heavily regulated banking community cannot waive account requirements, but Bob says his bank tries to find a way to help the "unbanked" develop a banking relationship and cultivate a credit score, without which they will always be a financial outsider. Not eligible for a checking account? Maybe the bank can set that person up with a prepaid debit card to serve as a first step up the financial ladder. It's a long way from a mortgage, but you've got to get your hand on the ladder before you can start climbing it.

Bob tells a story of a young single mother who got her banking start with a small-dollar-amount loan.

"She paid it off perfectly, and when she made her last payment, she brought her two young sons with her because she wanted them to see her paying off a loan at a bank.

That breaks the cycle! Now, she has a relationship with the bank—and her sons do, too," Bob says.

This is another feel-good story that would feel just as good if it took place in another time frame, say the dawn of the Civil Rights Movement or during the Great Recession. But it takes on added significance because it happened in the present day. Those two young boys, brought in to witness their mother's initiation into the credit-worthy world, are members of the current youngest generation, the one whose name has still not jelled—the group of people under the age of twenty-five that we variously call iGen or GenZ. These are people who were born into a world where internet banking always existed and was never a novelty. They see nothing weird about a faceless interface with a bank whose physical location is unknown to them. Because they will grow up knowing a brick-and-mortar bank that actually served—there's that word again—that actually *served* their family, their future inclinations in banking will have been shaped in childhood.

So, if you aspire to immunity from disruptors, focus on serving people by solving your customers' problems. You are not selling widgets; you are solving problems associated with widgets. It's how you validate the value of locking eyeballs with your customer. Serving people leads to more than a warm feeling—it leads to success.

WHAT WORKS

→ The values of the client, not the value of the product, are the basis for business relationships.

→ Relationships and stories drive customers' decisions as much as or more than product attributes.

→ If you focus on a single sale, that's what you get. If you create a connection, you'll get many more.

→ Consumers are driven by what they want more than what they need. You may know what they need—find out what they want.

→ Everyone enters the marketplace to solve a problem. Find their problem and solve it.

9

WORK HAPPY

Work's rewards are more than just a paycheck.

Listening to myself from my recent past can be either a humbling experience or a real ego boost. I've learned this from reviewing the initial two hundred episodes of my *What's Working* radio programs. For the most part, my interviews don't spend a lot of time staring into crystal balls, and for good reasons. When your predictions and forecasts are wrong, you come across as an intellectual lightweight. I prefer to stay firmly grounded in the present. But when I do make a prediction and it turns out right, hey, it's hard not to congratulate myself privately. And when I hit the mark with eerie precision, I surprise myself. I know that I know what I'm talking about, I know I have honed my business skills over the past thirty-plus years, but when I go out on a limb with a prediction and it is right on the money, it feels deeply satisfying.

That's what happened to me near the end of 2018. My guest was a boat manufacturer out of Indiana. I did a little research in advance on the labor challenges this fellow was facing, and I realized he and other manufacturers around him in one single county were resetting the table stakes for production work throughout the country. Maybe not at that very moment, perhaps, but in the very near future. And now, three years and one long pandemic later, those stakes have indeed changed.

Case Study

LET ME FLOAT AN IDEA BY YOU

SHOW TITLE: *Phil Smoker—Elkhart, Indiana—Historic Low Unemployment—and Making It All Work*
RELEASE DATE: *December 31, 2018*

But before I go into all that, let's go back to why this single county in Indiana is a bellwether for production employee expectations and what it can tell us about the workplace's role in worker happiness.

Elkhart, Indiana, is a city of a little more than fifty thousand people, and the city makes up about a quarter of the population of Elkhart County. A sizable chunk of the economy in Elkhart, both the city and the county, revolves around manufacturing, specifically manufacturing recreational vehicles or RVs. In fact, the area is touted as "the RV capital of the world." This little hotspot accounts for a whopping 80 percent—some estimates are even higher—of the RVs produced in this country. The list of RV producers based there is long, and you'll recognize some of these names even if you aren't part of the RV culture: Forest River, Keystone, Skyline, Sun Valley, Travel Supreme, Thor Motor Coach, Gulf Stream, Jayco. And that's not even a full list.

How seriously do these folks take their RV production? Well, when you go to the Elkhart Indiana Convention and Visitors Bureau's website, you can read up on the area's various attractions—which include scheduled public tours at multiple RV plants and the RV/MH (Recreational Vehicle and Manufactured Housing) Hall of Fame and Museum. That's taking the regional business really seriously!

My guest this particular episode was Phil Smoker. He's the vice president of sales at Starcraft/Smoker Craft, which manufactures several lines of boats—fishing boats to pontoon boats to deck boats, at all price points. More importantly, though, he's part of the fifth generation of his family to build boats in Elkhart.

Yes, boats, not RVs. While Elkhart may dominate the RV manufacturing world, it also produces other things, and manufacturers like Phil and his boat-building company wind up competing for the same employees who would otherwise be putting together luxury motorhomes. When I talked to Phil, the unemployment rate in Elkhart County was 2.4 percent—half that of the national figure at the time.

Now, if you've ever tried to pin down what the term "full employment" means, you know that's a tricky figure. The problem isn't that you can't find the answer—the internet is full of answers. The problem is you can't find the same figure twice. Casual news media references put it somewhere between 4 percent and 5 percent, figuring at that level anyone who wants a job can find one. Economists know it's significantly more complex than that, and the federal Bureau of Labor Statistics uses a complex formula that hinges on factors like inflation. But by any measure, a local employment rate of half the national unemployment rate is impressive, and it clearly means if you need to hire a boatbuilder or an RV assembler or anyone else with production skills, you've got your work cut out for you.

Meanwhile, functioning in this tight labor market, Phil's company is also growing—growing at a rate of about 20 percent a year since recovering from the 2008–2010 recession. It's enough to give a human resources department a massive headache. Smoker Craft has responded by aggressively improving the work environment—not just the dollars per hour, but by making time off generous and accessible, by upgrading restrooms and cafeteria facilities, by staging events involving workers' families, even by relenting on the current bugaboo of cell phones and earbuds in the workplace.

"With our history, we have a lot of longtime employees. We carry multiple generations of families working here over time," Phil says. "We value a lot of time off, and we try to schedule production so that people can actually take their time off. For our health care plan, we'll go beyond what other people are providing. We try to treat people as well as we can. At the same time, though, the environment is so competitive."

And in case you are wondering, Phil figures employers may not know it yet, but they've lost the war on personal devices in the workplace.

"Everyone talks about the Millennials," he says. "We allow them to use their earbuds and their phones—we figured out a way to do that. It was something they wanted and they needed. We talked about phones and how important it is that they have access to their phones at certain periods of the day. We're just trying to minimize the disruption of it while still giving them the freedom to use it."

The company has also discovered that fewer and fewer new hires are coming in with the needed trade skills, so they've hired a training team to bring them up to speed.

To get an idea of how far the worker accommodation has gone, consider this: Among the new amenities installed was a smoking area. Given the dynamics of tobacco in the public arena these days, I consider that huge. I mean, I know lots of companies that penalize smokers on their health insurance rates—and this company reinstitutes a smoking area!

As I introduced Phil to my audience three years ago, I told them they were about to hear about some amazing incentives to keep employees in place. And I made that prediction that turned out to be so spot-on: "The companies in Elkhart are paving the way for what will be normal in the workplace to come. They are a hotbed; they are a crucible. One of these days what they offer in these high-employment places will become standard in every corner of the nation."

A lot changed in the three years between that interview and this writing. COVID-19 came and stayed, two years and counting. Jobs disappeared overnight. But as we began to claw our way back, slowly and in fits and starts, a new phenomenon appeared. Employers couldn't find workers. Those incentives that folks in Elkhart employed pre-pandemic suddenly looked like smart moves in a post-pandemic world where people suddenly wanted more from a job than a paycheck. It'll take years of perspective and lots of study to fully understand the worker shortage that materialized as pandemic restrictions relaxed; but you definitely get the feeling that things have changed, permanently, and not just as we adjust to a new normal. Living and working in the shadow of a deadly plague has permanently altered attitudes toward the workforce.

Way back in 2018, Phil Smoker and his boat builders saw this coming. They had already shifted from an incentive program driven by production to one linked to longevity, because workers who stuck around for five, ten, twenty-five years were worth more to the company.

Today's Smoker Craft began in 1921 as a lumber company. Phil's great-grandfather began to build wooden boats with the excess wood, and eventually specialized in oars and paddles along with lumber. That aspect of the business was sold in the late 1990s. But the core business, after a stint that involved RVs, shifted specifically to aluminum fishing boats, eventually branching out into pontoons and fiberglass boats. Starcraft, another family-owned boat business, joined them in recent years to form today's company.

Now, it would be naïve to say the increased perks and freshly painted bathrooms override competition in wages. The company still goes head-to-head with fierce competition, and the main weapon is a higher wage.

"A gentleman who had been with us for about twenty-three years just recently left. He was here on our campus, and he took another job because he could make $10 an hour more. It was harder work, but that's hard to pass up. That's real money," Phil says. "But what we've found over the last six months, we've brought a lot of those people back who left for more money. They've come back due to the environment."

If you think politics makes strange bedfellows, you should see some of the odd relationships that come out of a tight labor market. For example, Elkhart County and its surrounding area has a significant Amish population. The combination of large families and increased land prices means fewer and fewer Amish men can support their families as farmers. Instead, the Amish are turning to the region's appetite for production workers. Amish men cannot drive in to work, but employers charter buses to collect them and deliver them in to work in Elkhart's industries.

"It's something we've definitely grown up with around here," Phil says.

Now, it's hard to offer someone something and then take it back—or try to—at a later date. So, once the workforce gets accustomed to certain standards, don't expect those standards to backslide, at least not without a fight. Companies that surrender on the use of personal devices in the workplace, for example, may make peace among their employees today, but lots of luck getting that genie back in the bottle if management ever wants to change that policy.

A clearer example of how you cannot go backwards on working conditions can be found in the 40-hour work week. Try to extend that week—and I'm talking about a purely theoretical scenario where people are *not* paid overtime after 40 hours—and you get a grasp of the enormity of rolling back workplace benefits and perks. Once something becomes an accepted norm, it doesn't retreat easily. Federal law set 40 hours as the work week in 1940 and no one has blinked since. Raise the table stakes—that is, the minimum point at which you can compete in a competitive situation—and they are raised until some extraordinary event unsettles things.

And that, my friends, is why I predict we'll see a kinder, gentler work environment when tight labor markets become the norm instead of part of a cycle.

Case Study

CHASING OUR HAPPINESS TAIL

SHOW TITLE: *Is It the Workplace's Job to Make Employees Happy?*
RELEASE DATE: *February 25, 2019*

How did we get here? How did we move from the world where our parents considered themselves lucky to have a job and coped with whatever conditions were associated with it, to a workplace where people want something considerably more from a job than a paycheck and they're willing to change employers to get it?

I do a lot of work with some of the youngest members of the workforce in my studies of generational differences. And this youngest generation says they want the workforce to make them happy. Older generations want money or security or status, all of which can lead to happiness, I suppose, but these fledgling employees want to be happy and believe that their job should make them so.

I am reminded of a story told to me by a friend who was serving as a mentor to a very promising young architect in New York City. This young woman was hitting all the right goals, on her way to a truly promising career in her chosen field. But she said she would gladly give it all up if she could just find some way to overcome the loneliness she felt.

Loneliness? Happiness? How did these become workplace problems or responsibilities? I tackled that question with Dr. Elise Labbé-Coldsmith, a veteran psychologist, to get a better handle on why people have begun to feel their happiness is the responsibility of their job. After all, if loneliness is driving disruptive turnover at your business, well, this actually *is* your business' problem.

Dr. Labbé-Coldsmith has been in the psychology field for thirty-two years and is professor emerita and former psychology department head at the University of South Alabama. She earned both her master's and her doctorate at Louisiana State University, and she agreed to come on my radio program to discuss this interesting and controversial topic.

"There's a lot of research that shows people who are happy in their work environment are more productive, they're healthier, they take less sick days. So in terms of the work environment, it is in the best interest of the manager, or whoever the leader is, to work toward trying to support people and helping them experience happiness, joy in the work environment," she says.

"Loneliness is becoming a greater problem, probably related to technology and the way we work today," she adds, pointing to examples from her own evolving work experiences where phone calls and knocks on office doors have become emails and texts.

Workplace training that focuses on improving communication and encourages personal interaction might be one remedy. But Labbé-Coldsmith is not yet ready to say all young people have fewer interpersonal skills, since that would vary depending on educational level and background.

"Part of it goes back to being able to take time to understand yourself and determine what it is you want, and to develop specific plans and goals to achieve those desires you have," she says. "If you wake up every day and just kind of fly by the seat of your pants, you are less likely to experience meaning, fulfillment—and happiness."

The psychologist sees reason for optimism when it comes to happier workplaces, however.

"More and more, there's a model of leadership called 'servant-leader,' and leaders who take that approach try to provide means and ways and strategies for their employees to be as good as they can be. When that happens, you are going to see greater happiness and greater resilience and better social well-being, as well as better physical and mental well-being," Labbé-Coldsmith says.

So I just had to ask, "Isn't all this groundwork for happiness something that should be taught in the home to children instead of in the workplace to adults?" And she reminded me of the importance of role modeling for our children, letting them see us as happy in our work and having a meaningful job. "We forget to talk to kids about why we are doing things," she said.

That got me thinking about some observations I had made about the most effective teams and leaders I have studied. The best teams, I have learned, are led by people who get to the meetings early, say half an hour before the meeting. They didn't get the jump on the agenda by starting early, and they certainly didn't rebuke those who showed up on time. Instead, those leaders were there to talk to their team members, to learn what they had done that weekend, to talk about other work topics that weren't on the agenda perhaps, all in a casual and nonthreatening environment. Then, when the appointed time came for the meeting, they got down to business. Pretty quickly, the team members learned the value of showing up early. The work may have happened in the meeting, but the important business of team building took place in those informal pre-meeting sessions.

Some of us may derive our happiness at work from our paycheck alone. After all, we would be pretty unhappy without one! But as the workplace evolves with ever more technology, we travel on a two-way street. On one side, an employer must step up its game to remain attractive to the best people. Those people, on the other side, must overcome hurdles presented by technology versus human contact to build relationships with their coworkers, all part of finding fulfillment in the work that fills our days.

WHAT WORKS

+ Happy workers are productive workers. And they stay.

+ Today's employees value community, meaning, and fulfillment in their work as much as material rewards.

→ Replacing employees is far more costly to a business than retaining them. Retention is worth the effort and expense.

→ We spend most of our waking hours at work. That many hours of unhappiness is unsustainable.

→ Remote and hybrid working arrangements, as well as work-life balance, are moving targets. Stay flexible and up to date on employee expectations.

10

BE STRATEGIC

*Plan to sustain your business
and pass it on.*

Is there an epidemic of spinelessness among the successor generations of family-owned businesses? Wayne Rivers, who has worked for more than three decades helping family-owned and closely held businesses plan succession, believes there is.

Kids these days—by which we mean working-age young adults and not actual children—don't want to work. Is that a myth perpetuated by the bitter elders of these "kids" or an actual fact? After hearing what Sid Sexton has learned while operating a highly successful business in a high-turnover field characterized by hard, hot, physical labor, you might join me in voting "myth" to that statement.

These two questions come from opposite ends of the economic spectrum: the family business with enough success and assets to be attractive to the grown children it has nurtured throughout their lives, and the entry-level hardscrabble new employee staring down decades of a working future without any silver-spoon advantages. Yet as far apart as these two situations might be, they illustrate the same principle: We all want to see a path to the future in our jobs. Whether the tunnel we face is narrow and chipped from granite or oak-paneled and upholstered, we all want to see a light at the end of it. And the workplace's failure to give us a clear vision of that light, whatever our vantage point, leads to things like counterproductive stalemates among feuding family members or unmotivated, underperforming workers who perpetuate the myth that work ethic is a cultural relic.

Case Study

MAN UP OR BOW OUT

SHOW TITLE: *Succession Plans for Family Business: "An Epidemic of Cowardice"*

RELEASE DATE: *March 12, 2019*

Let's start with those family-owned or closely held businesses that Wayne has studied since the early '90s. That time period coincides with the key working years of the Baby Boomers, born between 1946 and 1964, the largest demographic bolus ever to hit the population of the United States (until it was replaced by the Millennials, that is).

So, while Wayne's had his eye on them, the oldest of these Boomers have aged from forty-four to seventy-four, and the youngest from twenty-six to fifty-six. They're flanking the traditional American retirement age, and every day, another ten thousand of them hit that sixty-five-years-old milestone. No wonder succession-planning consultants like Wayne are busy.

Wayne, by the way, is the co-founder and president of The Family Business Institute and author of, among other books, *The Eight Building Blocks for Creating a Sustainable Closely Held Company*. Consider it a primer for successful entrepreneurs who like the idea of their business legacy outlasting them.

The Baby Boomer pioneers among family-owned businesses—that is, those who are first generation, the founders of the business—cut their teeth on American business during a fascinating time. They saw the dawn of the high-tech age. They may well have been the ones who decided when their businesses would install fax machines, sign on for toll-free phone numbers, dive into computer-controlled inventory. They saw the entry of women and the dawn of diversity in the workforce. Direct deposit, ATMs, the ubiquitous credit card, containerized freight, environmental regulation and accountability, the replacement of pensions with 401Ks—there's hardly an aspect of American business that hasn't changed radically during the working years of Baby Boomers.

The savviest among them, those who built significant companies with enough economic staying power to keep the interest of the next generation, tended to be hard-driving, take-charge sorts. Turning over power was never going to be easy for these folks, as many of their successors have learned the hard way.

That's what happened to a friend of mine. He was a successful businessman when his dad invited him to join the family firm, with an eye toward succeeding him as head of the business. The plan was nothing particularly original: a period of executive apprenticeship for the son, an announcement of a planned succession, complete with time line, and a future for the father with some influence as a board chairman while the son actually ran the business. So far, so good. My pal went to work in the family's company, and it looked for a while like the future was set.

Only it wasn't.

As the planned succession date approached, the dad postponed it again and again. Vendors and customers and employees became confused. Even more alarming, the patriarch starting stripping profits out of the company rather than reinvesting. My friend was faced with an uncertain and deferred future, despite the promises he was given, and when he finally takes charge of the company, it may well only be a shell of its former self.

Wayne didn't seem surprised when I told him that story. After all, he's heard variations on it repeatedly over the past thirty years.

"It's really typical of founding generations. It's usually the dads that start these businesses (given business practices of their times). These guys start businesses, and they start families at the same time. If they have three kids, they really have four kids because one of them is the business, and it is always the favored child. Always. Because that's where they get their psychological jollies, their strokes, and everyone wants that," Wayne says.

Fast-forward a few decades. The kids are now grown, and the business has matured. So has Dad. He's in his early seventies now, and his hearing is going, his energy is waning, he doesn't like to drive at night, Wayne points out.

"This is happening to this lion of a man. The business is his legacy, that's who he is. He can't control his declining health, but what can he control? By God, he controls the business. America is still a very egalitarian culture, but there is still one place where we have kingdoms, and that is the closely held business," Wayne says. "It's a heady place to be the head of a family-owned or closely held business."

Such cases, Wayne says, call for backbone from the successor generation—and it is frequently in short supply. As an example, he turned to my story of my stranded friend and his father who balked at transition.

"He needs to talk to his dad constructively and engage him as a peer, a businesslike peer, on neutral ground, and not in a CPA's or a lawyer's office, because those guys work for his dad. Rent a conference room," Wayne says. "My advice to the son: Polish up his resume and push it out into the broader world. Otherwise, he has no alternative than to be whipsawed by this aging father. Can he make that same money elsewhere without being basically a tool of his daddy? Without a fallback plan, he has no alternative. If you are not prepared to leave, you can't look your mom and dad in the eye."

Uncomfortable discussions? You bet. But Wayne can point to three highly successful people who bit the bullet, had the conversations and actually left the family business. In time, in each of those cases, the father came back to the son and asked him to return—only now it was the sons who could dictate the terms. For obvious reasons, he's not naming the people and their companies, but he shared some details: one turned $10 million in gross revenue into $650 million in the years following the hard-fought succession; one with $2 million in gross revenue went on to turn down a purchase offer of $70 million as insufficient; and the third moved from $40 million in gross revenue to over a billion, clearing $100 million in debt in the year before the interview.

"They didn't have to come back," he says of the three winning examples. "People with these kinds of business-building gifts were going to be successful anyway. There's an epidemic among successor generations in family businesses, and the epidemic is spinelessness."

For the record, Wayne's business has advanced enough in the past thirty years that he has staff consultants who deal with families with a bit more tact than what he just said. But he doesn't back down from his bluntness. I challenged him, asking what were the odds that this hard-nosed tactic worked for these three businesses, but failed for many others?

"The other 997 people have just waited for Mommy and Daddy to figure things out or have dealt with the mess Mommy and Daddy left behind," he responds.

What often results is a mess. He mentioned one memorable "overlawyered" case in which the founding generation set up multiple trusts, leaving their grown children with a situation in which they can only build wealth for their own children, not for themselves. "How demotivating is that?" is his question.

"They're just placeholders. This lack of courage among this next generation of family members has got to stop, or you end up in a wrinkly bed and you're the one who made it," Wayne says.

So, if fearfully avoiding the subject of succession is the way to do it wrong, what is the way to do it right? Wayne says there is a magic bullet, but one that people reject because they've heard it before. Just as diet and exercise are actual, workable ways to lose weight but not ones anyone wants to embrace, strategic planning is the way to navigate succession in a family-owned or closely held business, he says.

People who have hired consultants and left the resulting plan in a binder on the shelf in the boardroom believe that strategic planning doesn't work—and they're right, if you don't work the plan, he notes. Work it right and you get the two things that are the goal of every family business: business prosperity and family harmony.

"Strategic planning is useless without weekly execution. Weekly is the perfect time module for getting any plan done. A month is too long—things fall through the cracks. A day is too short—you could wake up with the flu. A week is the perfect unit of time for measuring business success. It's like putting a puzzle together. Fifty-two weeks, minus Christmas and New Year's, and you can actually predict your financial performance plus or minus 5 percent using this process, if you do it right," Wayne says.

What Wayne says next brings us back to the path through the tunnel that I wrote about at the first of this chapter. "If you've already got the journey laid out for everyone to see, you've got people on the same sheet of music," he says. Everyone sees a future role for themselves down that road, and that need for reassurance is met.

Case Study

MY CRYSTAL BALL SHOWS
YOUR FUTURE

SHOW TITLE: *The Name May Say Lawn and Landscape but It's Much Much More than That*

RELEASE DATE: *March 4, 2019*

So that covers how the founder and his sons and daughters come to grips with a need to see a future for themselves in the business. Let's turn the lens to the other end of the spectrum and ask how an entry-level laborer sees a future in his or her job, and how an employer who helps that laborer find a way to envision a future can actually break the cycle of churning employee turnover, even in an industry fraught with it.

For this example, let's visit Sid Sexton and Sexton Lawn and Landscape, based in Daphne, Alabama, and covering a large swath of coastal Alabama. It's hot, physical, outdoor work in a region where people mainline air conditioning as a matter of course. Jobs like this tend to have high turnover rates, and they're the breeding ground for the myth that "Kids these days don't want to work." I know it's a myth because Sid somehow seems to find—and keep—good people who grow his company.

I have some personal experience with basic landscaping in coastal Alabama. One of my first summer jobs was doing landscape maintenance at Spring Hill College in Mobile. I learned a lot that summer, including the location of every drinking fountain and water spigot on Spring Hill's campus and the fact that I don't like working outside. That long-ago summer experience helps me recognize that what Sid is doing is extraordinary.

"The secret," Sid says, "is, I think, my 'why.' My first jobs were landscape jobs for a local landscape company and a golf course, and then I took some courses in school and I loved it. I figured if I like it, I can convince other people to like it too. I'm just a green industry cheerleader. My personal 'why' is changing lives through business."

What Sid does is lay out, in writing, a clear path to promotion and pay raises for his employees, including a series of courses, tests and certifications. His passion for the landscape industry is front and center throughout the process.

"These are folks that were floating around in the service industry, like restaurant workers and bartenders. There's no future in it and they're not working toward something," Sid says. Instead, his program offers joy, satisfaction and a chance to impact lives.

"That's where joy comes from, from progress. Here's this course, here's this test; You passed it! They learn self-confidence and they develop, working outside with their hands and creating beauty in nature," he says. "My purpose in life is to give these people opportunity. Growth creates opportunity, and I just want these people to have someplace to move up."

New employees typically start out learning safety procedures, then move on to plant identification. "Many of these folks did not do particularly well in their school careers and were even told they were dumb," Sid says. "You see the lights come on when they overcome obstacles."

"Here's how we're different, here's where you start at the bottom and here's how you get to the top," he says, citing thirty-day, sixty-day and ninety-day goals. "Here's how you go from this pay level to that pay level. It's your responsibility and your free will to advance."

Employees advance to become foremen, supervisors and mentors to newer employees. After a while, the training advances to soft skills like leadership and management and on to what Sid terms "extreme ownership" of performance.

Sid describes himself and his company as a "Fifteen-year overnight success." And one of the satisfactions that goes with that success is his conviction that his company has become the employer of choice in its field.

Perhaps more clearly than in any other example I could imagine, Sexton Lawn and Landscape illustrates a deep longing of people to see their future in their work. His entry-level workers may be cutting grass in coastal heat and humidity, but unlike me in my short stint behind a professional lawn mower, they see something much more worthwhile than just the next water faucet ahead of them.

Once again, we have found a company whose business is a shell for something greater. On the surface, it appears Sid and his troops are cutting your grass. He'll tell you they're giving you back several hours each week that you would otherwise spend maintaining your lawn and trying to solve pest and drainage problems. But Sid is actually a leadership development guru with a taste for things that grow, like plants—and people.

Do you see the path to your future in your business? If you hope to hand your family business off to the next generation, can the next generation see that path? And what about your employees? In the beginning of a labor shortage that looks like it is likely to be around for a while, if "kids these days" don't want to work for you, maybe it's that they see no future for themselves in your company, and that should be a wake-up call for you.

WHAT WORKS

→ Teach your employees to train their successors. Then give them all a path forward.

→ Change is the only constant. How will your business adapt to an ever-shifting landscape?

→ Plan for sustainability. Your business is thriving now, but what will it take to keep that going in the future? Put it down in real numbers.

→ Careful planning is the way to make sure that what you have built is built to last.

→ Succession planning is essential for the long-term and multi-generational success and survival of a business.

EPILOGUE

This book is part of my COVID pivot. When the pandemic shut down air travel and in-person meetings, the livelihood that I'd relied on for twenty-plus years nearly evaporated in an instant. I was able to scratch and claw and used Zoom and Microsoft Teams and such to deliver my traditional generational content to clients across the country who had booked me for their live events but went virtual instead. However, as you know, the quick rebound we'd all predicted to happen after COVID hit never occurred. And just as my calendar began to show some signs of life again in 2021, Omicron stepped in and shut it back down. It's been tough, to put it mildly. Save a few old, loyal clients, business stopped.

Because of my years of *What's Working* interviews, I was able to revisit some of the advice my guests offered about what to do when disaster strikes your business. First, they all said in a matter of words, keep going. Don't stop. Carefully plan your steps, take calculated risks, but keep going. One thing that will certainly cause your business to fail, they said, was stopping and staying stopped. That inertia is a business coffin.

Next, ask what is controllable and what is out of your hands. My guests were all able to point to things that they could do, work on, change, influence, etc. They identified what their actions could affect and put their energies there. I can't control COVID, and I can't control the event planners and meeting restrictions on what had been my bread and butter for twenty years, and I can't control the public's fear of disease; but what is under my control?

Finally, what do I want to do? What is "lighting me up," as Stephen Cope says? Perhaps I should look at this as a big gift for me to hit Control-Alt-Delete and reboot myself. I had grown weary of being away from home, giving anywhere between sixty to eighty and, at times, a hundred speeches a year. The travel and hotels and being gone had lost its luster and, in fact, had led to what could have been a fatal pulmonary embolism one night in a hotel room near the Atlanta airport. My kids were all teenagers, and I wanted and needed to be more present at home. Maybe this extraordinary business disruption was a gift in disguise. An ugly, horrible, and frightening gift, but a gift all the same.

So, I took an inventory of what I can control, asked myself where my passions were, and got moving. The *What's Working* radio show was where my efforts began. I called the radio station in Mobile where *What's Working* was being broadcast and told the station general manager that I think I can help in this crisis by putting guests on the air who can help small business manage this disruption. For about six months every Tuesday and Thursday for an hour beginning at noon,

I interviewed two guests who offered small-business advice and one guest whose job was to offer motivational words to keep our spirits up. I felt I was helping.

I also added focus to my radio commentaries called *Keepin' It Real* that broadcast statewide Fridays on Alabama Public Radio. I tried to make them more inspirational and positive, hoping that the short three-minute broadcasts each week would find the ears of someone who needed a boost or a smile or a little giggle. Again, I felt I was helping.

I committed to a thorough website redo. I wasn't sure where the cash would come from, but I signed the agreement on faith that I'd find it. When COVID released its grip, I wanted to be ready to hit the speaking circuit again. I have no desire to do sixty, eighty, or a hundred dates a year anymore, but I think twenty-four is reasonable. And I want to focus my speaking topics on the things that inspire me today and help my audience. So much of what I've learned from my radio interviews about people, business, and trends in the workplace and marketplace is showing up in these presentations. I think this reboot will be the best thing that's ever happened to me and my business. My revenue may never be the same as it used to be, but I know I'll savor and appreciate my work in new ways, and I already find it more interesting and will be grateful for all of it—another lesson my *What's Working* interviews taught me.

And then there's this book. This book never would have happened had COVID not forced me to sit down and examine my resources and try to figure out what new and different things I could do to generate some income, and what role an external hard drive full of *What's Working* conversations could play in it. Two hundred interviews with business leaders must have some value other than its broadcast value. The interviews are a treasure chest of expertise and insight. They're an inventory of ideas and encouragement. So, I went to work organizing them into this book.

My COVID pivot is not unique to me; I'm not alone. We will begin seeing other people and companies' COVID pivots surfacing soon. Some pivots happened quickly and then faded. I think of Calagaz Printing in Mobile, who went from commercial printing to making face shields for hospitals when personal protective gear was hard to find. They're now back to their traditional knitting. But others, like me, will begin to reveal their COVID pivots as the marketplace returns to some semblance of a new normal. There will be technology breakthroughs that will begin to trickle down to end users like you and me. There will be new markets and new products we never even considered because of COVID. Some companies and businesses have flourished during COVID due largely to the extraordinary infusion of cash injected into our economy by the federal government via PPP loans, low-interest SBA loans, and so many other factors. This historic infusion of cash (combined with some global political uncertainty) has led to the predicted extraordinary inflation we are seeing and feeling right now as I write this. When the cash is spent and the corrections occur, these companies will have to figure out new ways to survive. And I want to be there to tell their stories through my *What's Working with Cam Marston* radio show and podcast. That's what it's all about. Capturing their stories, hearing their lessons, sharing their lessons with listeners, and applying their lessons to my own business where they fit.

Are there two hundred more episodes in my future? I don't know. I'll go where the winds and the market opportunities take me—another lesson from my *What's Working* interviews—and if the radio show is part of it then, yes, there are two hundred more. I know for certain that I'll continue to ask questions. I can't stop. It's a part of who I am. Because, after all, I have a curiosity problem . . .

ABOUT THE AUTHOR

 $\mathcal{C}$ am Marston is an author, advisor, radio talk show host, and top-rated keynote speaker on the trends shaping the workplace and marketplace. His presentations are informative, engaging, humorous, and full of concrete research that is tailored to his audience. Cam enlivens the data with anecdotes, tales from the real business world, attention-grabbing visuals, and quips that make the messages and actionable strategies memorable.

His original focus was on generational differences and their impact on the workplace and marketplace. Cam and his firm, Generational Insights, have provided research and consultation to hundreds of organizations, ranging from small businesses to multinational corporations, as well as to major professional associations. Cam's four books and countless articles describe and analyze the major generations of our time, explaining how generational workplace and marketplace preferences affect every aspect of business, including recruiting and retention, management and motivation, and sales and marketing.

Cam also records commentaries for Alabama Public Radio called *Keepin' It Real*. They're his humorous and inspirational observations of the world around him and have won both statewide and national awards. They have recently been converted into short, subscription-based videos to be used as inspirational and motivational weekly training content for the workplace.

Cam's expertise and acumen are the products of over twenty years of research and consultation across a wide range of industries. He has provided insight and advice to leadership at the some of the world's most prominent corporations, including Kaiser Permanente, Charles Schwab, BASF, Nestle, Schlumberger, Fidelity, Warner Brothers, ESPN, Qualcomm, RE/MAX and Eli Lilly. He has also offered presentations and consultations for the U.S. Department of Agriculture, the Internal Revenue Service, NASA and the U.S. Army, as well as for major professional associations such as the American Bankers Association, the Health Care Compliance Association, FMI/The Food Industry Association, the Financial Services Roundtable, and the Million Dollar Round Table.

Cam's perspectives have been featured in the *Wall Street Journal*, *The Economist*, *Investment Advisor*, the *Chicago Tribune*, *BusinessWeek*, *Fortune*, *Money*, and *Forbes*, as well as on *Good Morning America* and the BBC. He holds a Bachelor of Arts from Tulane University and is a native and resident of Mobile, Alabama.

Printed in the USA
CPSIA information can be obtained
at www.ICGtesting.com
BVHW041055100823
668430BV00004B/6